the
automated
architect

N Cross

Research in Planning and Design

Series editor Allen J Scott

1 Place and placelessness E Relph
2 Environmentalism T O'Riordan
3 The new urban economics H W Richardson
4 The automated architect N Cross

p Pion Limited, 207 Brondesbury Park, London NW2 5JN

the
automated
architect

N Cross

Pion Limited, 207 Brondesbury Park, London NW2 5JN

ISBN 0 85086 057 1

Printed in Great Britain

Preface

This monograph is concerned with the impact of computers on architectural design. It is written for fellow research workers, for students, and for architects (and perhaps other designers) who want to begin to understand this impact and to anticipate its effects. My purpose in writing it is to try to fill a gap in the literature on computer-aided design (CAD), which generally glosses over embarrassing questions such as whether CAD improves either the quality of the end product, or the quality of the designer's working life.

Some architects already make fairly extensive use of computers in design. In the main, these are the enthusiasts who have committed themselves to the computer, whatever its implications may be. For the vast majority of architects, the advent of computer systems in their work is still some time in the future. But that future presses ever nearer. As I write this, it is announced that a large, well-known firm of British architects has just invested (considerably) in a comprehensive, American, computer-aided architectural design system, thus already preempting a comment of mine towards the end of this book that "before long, large-scale, comprehensive systems will be being introduced in architectural practice".

The principal reason why this firm of architects is installing such a CAD system is that they see the system as "a very powerful tool which will increase throughput". The decision is clearly, and understandably, primarily a commercial one: the new system is installed because it increases efficiency and productivity. For similar reasons, any commercial organisation instals new capital equipment, and hence production processes become mechanized and automated.

What has prompted my own interest and research in CAD, which I have drawn together into this monograph, has been a concern to try to establish what the architectural design process will actually be like when it has been mechanized and automated. There seems to have been rather little concern for this in the CAD research field. The 'change agents'—the researchers, the systems analysts, the computer programmers—have enthusiastically stormed the architectural design process, armoured with the knowledge that they are the vanguard of progress.

Informed debate on such aspects of technological progress has, however, often been lacking in the architectural profession in the past. Instead, there has been a chaotic swinging to-and-fro of opinion on matters such as industrialised buildings and high-rise flats. What is needed is a more careful assessment of "progress" from the outset, and it is with this intention in mind that I have prepared this monograph, in the hope that the progress of computer-aided architectural design can be discussed, challenged and, where necessary, redirected.

Perhaps I should hasten to add, though, that this is not intended to be simply a counterattack on the change agents—I have been too long in one or another of their camps myself for it to be that. I am trying rather to suggest that the various 'threats' and 'promises' of computerization should be identified quite openly, and as far in advance as possible. Some of the 'promises'—such as the potential for deprofessionalizing the design process —I welcome; but the 'threats' (and often one person's threat is another person's promise) need to be known, too.

This monograph might, therefore, be interpreted as an attempt at a fairly elementary piece of technology assessment. The main findings of this assessment are that there seem likely to be some very large and wide-ranging *effects* arising from computerization of the design process, but that, paradoxically and to my surprise, the *effectiveness* of the computer as an aid to design seems to be rather limited. An explanation or resolution of this paradox is beyond the scope of my intentions here.

Since I hope (as I suppose most authors do) that this book will reach a fairly wide readership, it begins with an introduction to computer-aided design, so that even readers who may be unfamiliar with the topic, or with its recent developments, will have a reasonable understanding of the background to CAD and the current state of the art. This introduction begins with a general historical discussion of the impact of technological change on the design process. The more immediate background (over the last ten to fifteen years) of developments in systematic design and the arrival of CAD is then presented, and this is followed by a state-of-the-art review of computer-aided architectural design.

Part 2 of the book begins by comparing some of the sweeping claims that have been made for the power of CAD with the reality of CAD in practice—or what is known of the reality from evaluation of CAD systems. In fact, little evaluation ever seems to be conducted—particularly in terms of comparing human performance with machine performance—and I therefore had to embark on some of my own. These rather limited experiments in assessing the effectiveness of computer aids to design are presented in some detail, since they have not been published elsewhere.

Part 3 also includes discussions of experiments that some colleagues and I made in an attempt, through simulation studies, to step into the future to gain a more intuitive and realistic view of what CAD might be like. Having thus seen the future, I am not at all sure that it works. However, through these and other studies, it is possible, as I have attempted, to begin to map out the effects that CAD systems are likely to have both on the design process and on the individual designer.

In Part 4, I try to relate what we have learned of the shortcomings of CAD systems to the more general study of human–machine systems design, and the allocation of roles to humans and machines. Finally, I raise a series of questions on CAD systems design—both the larger, ethical kinds of question, and the smaller, more practical ones. These latter I have put into the form of a 'system checklist', which I hope not only CAD systems designers but also architects (and others) who are contemplating, or being presented with, a switch to CAD will find useful in ensuring that humans, as well as machines, are included in the system design criteria.

This monograph is a tentative and *anticipatory* assessment of CAD in architecture. Its intention is not to provide final answers, to offer conclusive proofs, to forestall controversy, to close debate, or to be a definitive work. Rather, I intend it to be the reverse of all these: to raise questions, to spark research, to stir controversy, provoke debate, and, before long, to be superseded. The new Pion series of monographs in *Research in Planning and Design* offers an eminently suitable context for its publication.

My research work in computer-aided design was started by John Chris Jones, and is to him and Chris Goodwin that the inspiration and encouragement for my initial experiments in simulating CAD systems should be credited. The subsequent development and interpretation of these experiments is, however, my responsibility. In my later work I have been helped by many other colleagues at the Design Research Laboratory, University of Manchester Institute of Science and Technology, but especially Denis Harper and Reg Talbot. It have also had considerable and invaluable assistance from Tom Maver at the Department of Architecture and Building Science, University of Strathclyde. Allen Scott, editor of the Series, and John Ashby of Pion made many useful comments that led to the improvement of the manuscript for this book. Kitty Gleadell has patiently typed and retyped the various drafts.

Finally, this book is dedicated, not to the machines, but to the humans.

Nigel Cross
The Open University
1976

Acknowledgements

The author and publishers are grateful to the following for permission to reproduce their work:

The Architecture and Building Aids Computer Unit, Strathclyde University, for illustrations of the SPACES computer-aided design system.

William Collins Sons and Co Ltd and Michael Frayn for extracts from *The Tin Men* (Fontana Books, London, 1966), copyright © 1965 by Michael Frayn.

Professor W T Singleton for the table of "Relative advantages of clerks and computers" from *Man–machine Systems* Penguin Books, Harmondsworth, Middx, 1974).

Contents

Part 1 An introduction to computer-aided design

1 Design and technological change

1.1	Introduction	3
1.2	Postindustrial design?	3
	1.2.1 System design	4
	1.2.2 Design failures	5
1.3	Craft design	6
	1.3.1 Form and function	6
	1.3.2 Evolutionary design	7
1.4	Professional design	8
	1.4.1 Industrialization	8
	1.4.2 Self-conscious design	11

2 Systematic design

2.1	Design methods	12
	2.1.1 Methods of systematic design	12
	2.1.2 Design method in architecture	16
2.2	The design process	17
	2.2.1 Design research	17
	2.2.2 Cyclical structures	18
	2.2.3 Hierarchical structures	19
	2.2.4 Two-dimensional structures	21
2.3	The development of computer aids	24
	2.3.1 The CEDAR system	25
	2.3.2 The Harness system	26
	2.3.3 The West Sussex system	27
	2.3.4 Computer graphics	28

3 Computer-aided design

3.1	Computer analysis	29
	3.1.1 Hierarchical trees	29
	3.1.2 CLUSTER	30
	3.1.3 MDS	32
	3.1.4 AIDA	32
3.2	Computer synthesis	33
	3.2.1 The Whitehead and Eldars program	35
	3.2.2 Minimum house plans	37
	3.2.3 STUNI	38
	3.2.4 BAID	39
	3.2.5 CEDAR	40
3.3	Computer evaluation	40
	3.3.1 INTU-VAL	41
	3.3.2 PACE	41
	3.3.3 URBAN5	42
	3.3.4 COPLANNER	43
	3.3.5 City-Scape	44

A*

3.4	An integrated example	46
	3.4.1 SPACES 1	46
	3.4.2 SPACES 2	48
	3.4.3 SPACES 3	51
3.5	The machine as architect	56
	3.5.1 The machine as hero	56
	3.5.2 The machine as villain	57

Part 2 Humans versus machines

4 Human–computer interaction

4.1	The symbiotic partnership	63
	4.1.1 Interactive systems	64
4.2	Evaluation of computer systems	65
	4.2.1 Response time	65
	4.2.2 On-line vs off-line	66
	4.2.3 Evaluation of solutions	68
4.3	Comparison of human and machine performances	68
	4.3.1 A queuing problem	69
	4.3.2 A building design problem	69
	4.3.3 A travelling salesman problem	70
4.4	A computable design problem	71
	4.4.1 Room layouts	72

5 The effectiveness of computer aids

5.1	Man versus machine	74
	5.1.1 Experimental design	74
	5.1.2 Results	77
	5.1.3 Discussion	84
5.2	Man versus man–machine versus machine	85
	5.2.1 Experimental design	85
	5.2.2 Results	89
	5.2.3 Discussion	92

Part 3 Anticipating the future

6 Simulation of computer-aided design systems

6.1	Technology assessment	105
	6.1.1 Forecasting change and effect	106
	6.1.2 Systemic testing	106
6.2	Simulation studies	108
	6.2.1 An information retrieval system	109
	6.2.2 An intelligent system	110

7	**The effects of computer aids**	
7.1	Effects on the individual designer	112
	7.1.1 Stress	112
	7.1.2 Intensification of work rate	113
	7.1.3 Reduction of staff	114
	7.1.4 New tasks	114
	7.1.5 Threats and promises	115
7.2	Effects on the design process	116
	7.2.1 Briefing	117
	7.2.2 Production information	119
	7.2.3 The management pyramid	119
	7.2.4 The change agents	121
	7.2.5 Roles and relationships in the building team	121
	7.2.6 User participation	123

Part 4	**Design systems design**	
8	**Human and machine roles in design**	
8.1	The need for assessment	129
	8.1.1 Effects and effectiveness	129
	8.1.2 Lack of knowledge	130
	8.1.3 Inadequate reporting	131
	8.1.4 How difficult is designing?	132
8.2	Man–machine systems design	133
	8.2.1 Allocating functions	134
	8.2.2 Positioning the interface	137
8.3	The allocation of roles	138
	8.3.1 Strategies and tactics	138
	8.3.2 System design concept	139

9	**Questions for design systems**	
9.1	The design of design	140
	9.1.1 What is designing?	140
	9.1.2 Magic versus hackwork	141
	9.1.3 The power of the system designer	142
	9.1.4 The design of design systems	143
9.2	System checklist	144

Appendix	148
References	155
Classified bibliography	163
Author index	173
Subject index	175

Part 1

An introduction to computer-aided design

"Professional football is becoming increasingly uneconomical, but the pools industry has to carry on somehow. It doesn't take even the stupidest wee businessman long to see that paying twenty-two men to do nothing but make a random choice between win, lose, and draw is economic madness. Once you've done football it won't take people long to see that you can replace all the racecourses in the country with one quite simple and inexpensive computer. And of course cricket. When takings at the gate have fallen low enough to cure any tendency to sentiment, people will notice that a computer is a far more suitable tool than a cricket team for producing a complex score sheet from the variables of ground moisture, light, surface wear on ball, fallibility of wicket-keeper, and so on. In fact all the complex mass of statistics produced by the sports industry can without exception be produced not only more economically by computer, but also with more significant patterns and more amazing freaks....

"...I think we can assume that a computer is a more efficient statistic-producing machine than any possible combination of horses, dogs, or muscular young men. But that's not the end of it. For what have we shown? That any human activity which consists of repetition, or of manipulating variables identifiable in advance according to predetermined rules, or of manipulating a known range of variables at random, can in theory at any rate be performed by a computer."

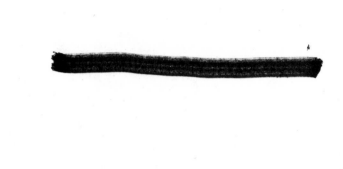

Design and technological change

1.1. Introduction

The concept of the machine seems to have dominated architectural design philosophy in the twentieth century. Every architect knows Le Corbusier's slogan of the 1920s: "a house is a machine for living in", and many will also have heard of 'the architecture machine' of half a century later (Negroponte, 1970).

Although the 'machine for living in' and the 'architecture machine' may appear to share a common philosophical heritage, they actually represent very different concepts of the role of the machine in architectural design. For Le Corbusier the machine was a source of aesthetic inspiration; he was concerned primarily with the architectural *product*, which he wanted to look like, feel like, and be constructed like a machine. However, the 'architecture machine' relates primarily to the architectural *process*; it is a machine for designing, a computer which might have a human partner, but which might also be a designer in its own right.

This contrast between the machine as architecture and the machine as architect illustrates a radical shift in concerns within the design professions that developed in the 1960s. Perhaps it would be more accurate to say that the shift in concerns happened within the design schools, if not necessarily within the professions as such. In architecture for example the design process very suddenly became a major teaching and research topic, but the vast majority of architects continued to rely on the traditional design skills that they had acquired by painstaking practice and apprenticeship.

Nevertheless the teaching and research have grown and so too, slowly, has the application of the new knowledge. In particular the application of the computer as a design aid has been a significant development that has been promising (or threatening) to make a major breakthrough into architectural practice for some time. Such a major breakthrough would go beyond the minority of enthusiast architects who already use computers, to a situation in which computer-aided architectural design is regarded as a commonplace. That would be a radical change not only for architects, but also for their colleagues in associated professions, for builders, for building clients, and perhaps for every building user. It could mark the emergence and recognition of a new 'machine age' in design.

1.2 Postindustrial design?

"If one speculates on the shape of society forty or fifty years from now, it becomes clear that the 'old' industrial order is passing and that a 'new society' is indeed in the making. To speak rashly: if the dominant figures of the past hundred years have been the entrepreneur, the businessman, and the industrial executive, the 'new men' are the scientists, the mathematicians, the economists, and the engineers of the new computer technology."

Thus Daniel Bell (1967) announced a new, 'postindustrial' society. He may indeed have been speaking rashly, but he is not alone in his basic belief that a new form of society is emerging in the technologically advanced nations. This belief developed widely during the period from the early 1960s to the early 1970s. McLuhan (1964), Galbraith (1967), Toffler (1970), Schon (1971), and Bell (1974), amongst others, mapped the patterns of industrial, technological, and social changes that are generally regarded as indicative of emerging postindustrialism. These patterns include changes in the established structures of employment and leisure, of production and consumption, of knowledge and communication, and of planning and personal life-styles.

Of course there is considerable debate surrounding the idea of 'postindustrial society' and whether or not it exists or is coming to be and, above all, its exact nature. The concept of a postindustrial society is regarded with either enthusiasm or dismay by different people. The enthusiasts herald it as a society in which everyone is liberated from the constraints of industrialization, whereas the pessimists suspect that it will be nothing other than a more advanced form of 'one-dimensional' (Marcuse, 1964), 'technological' (Ellul, 1964), or 'technocratic' (Roszak, 1970) society.

Significantly the decade from about 1963–1973 also saw the emergence of new concepts of design and the design process, particularly in architectural design. There was the emergence of new design methods (Jones and Thornley, 1963; Broadbent and Ward, 1969; Jones, 1970) and computer aids to design (Campion, 1968; Negroponte, 1970; Auger, 1972), new approaches to the concept of architecture (Weeks, 1965; Habraken, 1972), and new attitudes towards participation in the design process and the role of the professional designer (Cross, 1972b; Goodman, 1972). Do these developments signal the emergence of postindustrial design?

1.2.1 System design

Schon (1969) has argued that the transition to postindustrial society would inevitably bring about a revolution in design. He suggests that "From the point of view of design... this transition has deep implications which we can already feel. It forces a virtual revolution in our concepts of the design process and the design profession". The most important feature of the transition that Schon draws to the attention of designers is a series of shifts in the concerns of industry; from product to process, and from component to system.

An example of these shifts would be that of a business corporation recognizing that it should diversify from producing, say, motorcars, to producing transportation systems; or from houses to shelter systems. The implications for the designer are clear; he will be called upon to generate systems innovations, rather than just product modifications. Schon suggests that designers will have to become systems designers, and that systems design will become 'a central corporate function'.

To some critics, the idea of design becoming 'a central corporate function' will sound alarming. It sounds like the fulfilment of the technocracy, with the experts (the designers) and the businessmen in joint control of technological change, and their aims being the aims of the modern corporation: economy, efficiency, production, and indiscriminate consumption.

Jones (1970), a leading advocate of new approaches to design, also sees design being extended to 'systems design', although he offers a slightly different analysis from that of Schon's for the 'need for new methods'. His starting point is not so much that a changing social and industrial context is presenting new opportunities for the evolution of the design process, but that the conventional design process ('design-by-drawing') seems to be creating as many problems as it does solutions.

1.2.2 Design failures

Jones suggests that a notable limitation of the scale drawing (the principal design method of industrial society) is that it is a very weak model of the product-in-use situation. The scale drawing is a means of designing a product in isolation from its manufacture and use, and although this was once an advantage (to the manufacturer) it now begins to present disadvantages (to the user). For example, incompatibilities may arise between different products which a user wants to combine, or when a product is used on a mass scale (for example the mass use of the motorcar). These are what Jones calls the *external* compatibilities of a product. The scale drawing resolves only *internal* compatibilities, such as the relative locations, dimensions, etc of separate components of the product.

With the scale drawing as virtually his only design method or design aid, the designer has to rely extensively on his experience and imagination to foresee the external requirements and implications of his design. In novel situations, such as designing in new materials or for new environments, his experience may well be irrelevant and his imagination inadequate. So the conventional design process seems to have a major and increasingly important shortcoming, that of failing to deal adequately with external compatibilities.

To these 'external' failures must be added the 'internal' failures that we have perhaps come to take for granted. In architectural design, this has meant buildings that have been too hot, too cold, too wet, too noisy, too dangerous, too expensive, or just too inadequate to live in comfortably.

The design process is therefore under considerable pressures for change. These pressures include the criticisms of design failures, the development of new design methods (including computer-aided design), the introduction of a wider range of participants, and the general contextual changes of social, industrial, and technological progress. Most of these pressures originate from outside the design professions and are not under professional control. Understandably, many professional designers are defensive of their established design privileges, but we should remember that these established processes and privileges do not have a terribly long history, and that they properly belong to industrial society and not necessarily to postindustrial society.

1.3 Craft design

Although man has always been a designer, there have not always been men called designers. The activity which is now conventionally regarded as design—carried on in special places, by special means, and by special people whose job it is to be designers—is a comparatively recent phenomenon in Western history. So we should perhaps not be too surprised if this special activity comes, as it is doing, under pressure for change; there is really nothing sacrosanct about the trinity of the design office, the drawing board, and the professional designer. Neither need we necessarily be dismayed if this trinity is broken up by the pressures for change, fearing that the quality of design might suffer if it loses some of its specialisms. As Jones (1970) has pointed out: "Neither the professional designer, nor the drawing board upon which parts of a design can be adjusted relative to each other, are essential to the evolution of complex forms that are well fitted to the circumstances in which they are used".

Jones reaches this conclusion from a study of the preindustrial craft process, which seems to have been a particularly reliable process of developing good designs. Most modern designers regard the majority of genuinely craft-made objects as things of beauty, astonishingly well-adapted to the requirements of their making and using. Yet the complexities of these objects are often masked in a deceptive simplicity of form. Indeed it is often only when a traditional form is departed from in a new design that we become aware of the virtues and hidden subtleties of the old form.

1.3.1 Form and function

An example of this hidden complexity in craft-made forms is revealed in Thor Heyerdahl's account of his experiences of sailing the Atlantic in *Ra*, a papyrus boat, the design of which was derived from ancient Egyptian reed boat forms (Heyerdahl, 1971). Heyerdahl was demonstrating that it was feasible for such boats to have crossed the Atlantic, perhaps thus linking the ancient cultures of Egypt and Mexico. The design of *Ra* was copied (almost exactly) from ancient Egyptian wall paintings.

Heyerdahl recounts his discovery, early in the voyage, of the complexities hidden in one elegant feature of the boat, its tall inward-curled stern:

"Everyday we looked admiringly at the broad, in-turned curl on the high-peaked stern. What purpose did it serve? We placed no reliance on the general conviction that this curl was simply intended to beautify the shape of a river boat. Yet as the days passed we were as unable as the Egyptologists to detect any practical function for it whatever.

"We did constantly make sure however, that the curl was not beginning to straighten out. It remained in perfect shape, so our friends from Chad seemed to have been right in thinking that they had done their work so thoroughly that it would keep its curve without having to be fastened to the deck by rope."

The 'friends from Chad'—craftsmen boat builders, but with no remaining craft knowledge of this type of boat—had omitted a rope tie on the stern which had featured in the wall paintings. Gradually, the stern of the boat sank lower into the sea. More water washed in every day, and Heyerdahl considered sawing off the weighty upper part of the now sodden tail. Then suddenly he realized that the elegant tail had been no extravagance:

"The peculiar arch over the afterdeck was not built for beauty. The rope, which everyone thought would serve only to hold the cocked tail in tension, had a completely different function. The cocked tail stood by itself. The rope was not intended to pull the tail-tip down, but the afterdeck up. The high harp-shaped stern was meant to act as a powerful spring... We tied the bowstring in position, but it was too late now... We were the sufferers because we, like all the others, had assumed the peculiar arch of the tail to be the ancient boat designers' end, whereas it had been their ingenious means".

The integration of ends and means, of function and form, has of course been the avowed aim of the Modern Movement in design. So it seems that the highest ideal that the modern designer strives for is no more than that which was presumably taken for granted in an earlier 'design' process. And that process had in fact none of the features that we now associate with the modern design process. There was no professional designer; the craftsman carved and built directly in the appropriate material, to a 'design' that he had learned as an apprentice. There were no design drawings; the form of the object was itself a record of how all such objects should be formed. There was no design office, but an intimate link between the craftsman, his workshop, the user, and the place of use.

1.3.2 Evolutionary design

The craft process of developing well-fitting forms is said to have been similar to that of the evolution of the forms of organisms in nature; that is, a process of very gradual adjustment over a very long time. This evolutionary process eventually brought forth a form for the craft-made object which was well-suited to its functional requirements, as the form of an organism is well-suited to its environment.

Alexander (1964) has used a basically similar analogy of organism and environment to explain what he means by the 'goodness of fit' of a form to its function or 'context'. When perfect 'fit' between form and context is not achieved, then 'misfit' situations occur. These may occur either because the form was not originally adequate, or because the context has changed.

The craft process achieves good 'fit', according to Alexander, by response to, and the gradual elimination of, 'misfit' situations. In conjunction with this process of constant, purposeful adaptation there is a strong inhibition of wilful change. Taking his examples from traditional house-building processes, Alexander points to the rigidity of the 'unspoken' rules of these processes. There is, he says, "a wealth of myth and legend attached to building habits... Descriptions of the house, its form, its origins, are woven into many of the global myths which lie at the very root of (primitive) culture.... More forceful still... are rituals and taboo connected with the dwelling". And the clearest rigidity of tradition is manifested where builders are forced to work within definitely given limitations, such as specified types of wood, specified construction sequences, and specified shapes.

Alexander suggests that the two complementary aspects of the craft process—on the one hand strong resistance to overall change, and on the other a ready response to minor inadequacies—ensure its success. Furthermore the individual craftsman requires no highly creative abilities. His contribution to the process of adaptation is merely that he attempts (sometimes successfully) to correct 'misfits', which are themselves easy to recognize. Yet this apparently undemanding process was capable of generating design solutions of such integrity that to change or omit one feature could mean failure of the whole design.

We may not wish to return to the rigidities of the craft process, but this review of it does serve, I hope, to remind professional designers that the modern design process which they now know and love so well is not the only process capable of generating good design.

1.4 Professional design

The professional process of design in its familiar drawing-board form of today began to replace the craft process at about the same time as all the other features of industrialization replaced craftwork. The development of the modern process of design was one of the organizational changes which accompanied the many other changes in technology during Western industrialization.

'The drawing office' is now an essential feature of any large industrial concern; it takes its place amongst all the specialized offices which are complementary to the factory. The activity of design is an integral function of the industrial process, and the professional designer is a specialist, just like any other office worker and just like any other production worker.

1.4.1 Industrialization

The development of a professional design process fits rather neatly into the larger, historical process of industrialization. For example the introduction of the factory system of production meant that the craftsman was no longer an independent agent; he was thus unable to negotiate and discuss with his client the specific features of whatever object he was commissioned to produce. This design function therefore had to be taken over by someone else, who took instructions from the client, reformulated them, and passed them on to the production worker.

The hallmark of the industrialized production system is the fragmentation of tasks, or the 'division of labour'. Each specialized task produces only one part of the final, complete product. There is therefore a need for a formalized method of, first, splitting the whole product into components and, second, ensuring that these components when made will indeed recombine into the final product. This formalized method is embodied in the design drawings, which can specify each component accurately and also its immediate relationships to other components.

Formally splitting the final product into small components not only facilitates the division of labour, but also paves the way for mechanization. Each component can now be considered in terms of how best it can be manufactured, and it can be designed to suit the manufacturing process.

The new design process in fact can readily take into consideration new design criteria, such as the manufacturing process (as in design for mechanization), the distribution process (design for ease of packing and transport), the sales process (design for display), and the demands of industrial and business economics (design for the multiple use of standard parts, design for obsolescence). And the design process can itself of course be centralized in the head office, as are other functions of the firm.

The professional process of design has two very strong features which make it an essential part of the overall pattern of industrialization. These are:

1. It separates designing from making. This separation undermines the craftsman's previous autonomy and authority in his work, but it is a necessary aspect of the factory system and that system's subsequent development.

2. It provides, in its use of drawings, a formalized method for the abstract consideration of form. This method enables new forms to be devised and to be tested in a modelled form before, and quite separately from, the processes both of production and of use. The testing can be either rational, for example plotting the locus of a moving part, or intuitive, for example imagining the movement of occupants through the plan of a building.

This conventional modern design process did not of course spring into being overnight as the willing accomplice of the Industrial Revolution. Broadbent (1973) has noted that design drawings of a kind have existed since at least 2800 BC. Many of the significant features of the professional design process were developed during the Renaissance, for instance the sophisticated use of drawings and the cultivation of the expression of the designer's individuality in his designs. However, the design process as we know it today is clearly a significant feature of the wider process of industrialization.

Table 1.1. A summary of the main contrasting features of craft design, professional design, and a possible 'postindustrial' design process.

Craft design	Professional design	Postindustrial design
Produces objects well-adapted to their patterns of use (good 'fit' between form and 'context')	produces objects that may have shortcomings in their 'external compatibilities' between form and context	aims to understand 'goodness of fit' so as to recapture good fit between form and context
Suited only to a static, or very slowly changing, design context	introduced to try to cope with sudden, extreme changes in context	recognizes the existence of continual, rapid, contextual change
Emphasis on producing the single, 'correct' form to suit the needs of its context	emphasis on producing a wide range of 'experimental' forms, some of which may survive	emphasis once again on producing the 'correct' fit between form and context—but at the first attempt
Context was well-known; forms are rigorously designed to fit	context is poorly understood; forms are loosely designed to fit	context and form are analyzed and designed together
Long time scale of 'design process'	short design time scale	relatively longer time scale, with more attention to analysis before designing begins
'Evolutionary' design process based on real-world, trial-and-error interaction between form and context	'design-by-drawing' process in which forms are modelled and tested before manufacture	requires new design process, probably using design methods, computer aids, etc
Unwritten rules of design, maintained by firm traditions and the passing on of craft knowledge through apprenticeship system	mixture of guesswork and understanding, utilizing scientific and technical knowledge within a largely intuitive design process	formulation of explicit design rules will depend on sophisticated information-processing systems as aids to rapid learning for each specific design task
Little separation of roles; client/designer/maker/user could be one person	separation of roles; designer one specialist amongst many	fragmentation of design function amongst researchers, information scientists, social scientists, production technologists, design methodologists, etc
Anonymous 'designers'	stress on the designer's individuality	anonymous design teams
Constant minor adaptations to the form of the artefact during use	redesign of complete new artefacts to correct for shortcomings	major adjustments to artefacts designed for flexibility; design-in-use philosophy
Dealt only with 'components' level of design	deals with design of 'components' and 'products'	will deal with 'system' and 'process' levels of design

1.4.2 Self-conscious design

The Industrial Revolution brought not only the desire and ability to design and make larger artefacts and to produce these artefacts more rapidly than before, but also the development of new materials for use in manufacture, the stimulation of demand for new products, and the recognition of new human and social requirements. To all these changes in 'context' the response was the development of a 'self-conscious' design process (Alexander, 1964).

Unlike the craft process, however, a guarantee of good design is not built into the 'self-conscious' professional process. There are many, more or less obvious, design failures experienced in everyday modern life—from the eye-level grill that spits hot fat in your eye, to the motorway fog disasters—that bear witness to the shortcomings of conventional design procedures.

This lack of success in modern design, the limitations of the professional design process, and the apparently still-accelerating cultural 'context'—increasingly rapid rates of technological change—have led to the search for a new design process, which would use new methods and new aids. Many design teachers and design researchers, perhaps even a few designers themselves, suspect that 'design-by-drawing' is no longer wholly adequate, and that a radical mutation is now required in the evolution of the design process. (See table 1.1 for a comparison of 'postindustrial' design with professional and craft design.)

Systematic design

2.1 Design methods

Examples of, and proposals for, new design methods began to appear in
the early 1960s, often as developments from the operational research
techniques that originated in the Second World War, and hence often
designated 'systematic' methods. The most significant event in the early
history of design methods was the Conference on Design Methods held in
London in 1962 (Jones and Thornley, 1963). The publication of the
proceedings of this conference was an early stimulus to the establishment
of 'design methods' as an academic subject. However, there had been
earlier manifestations of an interest in 'scientific design', notably at the
Hochschule für Gestaltung (HfG) at Ulm, West Germany.

Perhaps two contributions to the 1962 conference subsequently received
the most attention. One was Page's (1963) comment in his review of the
papers that "there only seems to be one common point of agreement, and
that is that systematic design is a three stage process, demanding analysis,
synthesis and evaluation". Page qualified his own belief in such a clear-cut
process, but his qualifying remarks have been largely ignored. The second
contribution that received a lot of attention was Jones's (1963) "Method
of Systematic Design". (A third popular contribution was Alexander's,
1963, "Determination of components for an Indian village" but that
achieved even greater popularity when it was subsequently published in his
Notes on the Synthesis of Form, 1964.)

2.1.1 Methods of systematic design

Jones' Method of Systematic Design was an attempt at "a unified system of
design... aimed particularly at the area that *lies between* traditional
methods, based on intuition and experience, on the one hand, and a
rigorous mathematical or logical treatment, on the other" (my emphasis).
So, from the very beginning, systematic design was not meant to be a
replacement of intuition by logic, but a synthesis of the two: this is much
the same argument that has been used subsequently in connection with
the development of computer-aided design processes. This synthesis was
to be achieved in the Method of Systematic Design by recognizing that all
the logical activities should be *externalized* into charts, diagrams, lists,
specifications, etc, so that the designer's mind could be left "free to
produce ideas, solutions, hunches, guesswork, at any time..."

The complete stages of Systematic Design were listed as:
1 Analysis:
   1.1 Random list of factors,
   1.2 Classification of factors,
   1.3 Sources of information,
   1.4 Interactions between factors,

1.5 Performance specifications,
1.6 Obtaining agreement;
2 Synthesis:
   2.1 Creative thinking,
   2.2 Partial solutions,
   2.3 Limits,
   2.4 Combined solutions,
   2.5 Solution plotting;
3 Evaluation:
   3.1 Methods of evaluation,
   3.2 Evaluation for operation, manufacture, and sales.

Thus the Method of Systematic Design looked very much like a set of step-by-step procedures based on a three-stage process of analysis–synthesis–evaluation, despite Jones's intention "to leave the mind free" and despite Page's warnings that the design process would be in practice much more of an iterative muddle than it appeared to be in the clean lines of a theoretical three-stage process. These intentions and warnings were often overlooked by the enthusiasts (often design students) who tried to take up 'systematic design' in the perhaps not unreasonable expectation that it would mean a design process that was logical and rational—in a word, systematic. (See table 2.1 for a summary of various definitions of the stages of the design process.)

Indeed it was not long before a much more rigorous Systematic Method for Designers was being developed by Archer in a series of articles in *Design* magazine during 1963–1964 (Archer, 1965). This 'systematic method' consisted of seven main stages: briefing, programming, data collection, analysis, synthesis, development, communication. Together these contained over two-hundred activities, which were listed in terms of a very cool logic but with little or no advice to the designer on how to perform the often difficult tasks.
For example:
5.2   postulate means for reconciling divergent desiderata in performance specification;
5.2.1   examine the augmented performance specification prepared under 5.1.20, and identify and group those desiderata which appear to be interrelated;
5.2.2   list the groups of interrelated desiderata;
5.2.3   from the list prepared under 5.2.2, select those groups containing desiderata which appear to be divergent or contradictory;
and so on.

A detailed step-by-step procedure for engineering design had been developed earlier by Asimow (1962). He called his procedure "the morphology of design", which "refers to the study of the chronological structure of design projects. It is defined by the phases and their constituent steps". The phases of this morphology were given as:

Table 2.1. "Systematic design is a three-stage process, demanding analysis, synthesis and evaluation" (Page, 1963). Some of the definitions which have been given for these three stages.

Definition

Analysis	Synthesis	Evaluation	Source
Listing all design requirements and reducing these to a complete set of logically related performance specifications	finding possible solutions for each individual performance specification and building up complete designs from these with least possible compromise	evaluating the accuracy with which alternative designs fulfil performance requirements for operation, manufacture, and sales before the final design is selected	Jones (1963)
Clarifying of goals; identifying problems, nature of difficulties; exploring relationships; producing order from random data	creating part-solutions; combining part-solutions into consistent and feasible overall solutions; generating of ideas	(appraisal) applying checks and tests; applying criteria, constraints, and limits; selecting of 'best' solution from a set; testing for consistency	Markus (1967)
Collecting and classifying all information relevant to the design problem on hand	formulating potential solutions to parts of the problem, which are feasible when judged against the information contained in the analysis stage	attempting to judge by use of some criterion or criteria which of the feasible solutions most satisfactorily answers the problem	Luckman (1967)
Breaking the problem into pieces	putting the pieces together in a new way	testing to discover the consequences of putting the new arrangement into practice	Jones (1970)

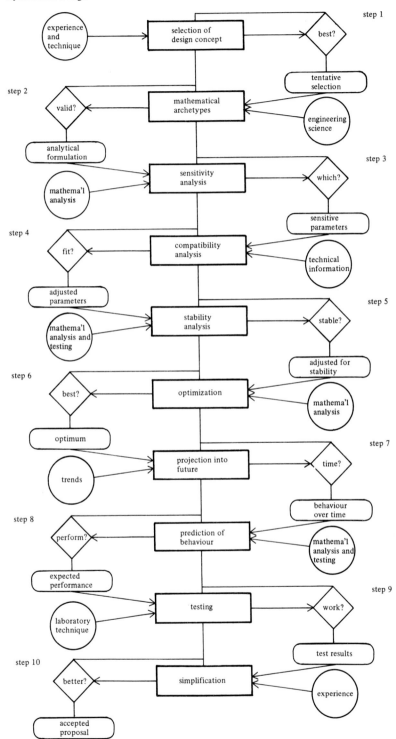

Figure 2.1. Asimow's (1962) flow chart for the preliminary design phase.

Primary design phases:
   1. feasibility study,
   2. preliminary design,
   3. detailed design.
Phases related to production–consumption cycle:
   4. planning for production,
   5. planning for distribution,
   6. planning for consumption,
   7. planning for retirement.
For each of the primary design phases Asimow gave a detailed breakdown
of their constituent steps, which was backed up with flow charts showing
the iterative decision loops (figure 2.1).

This systematization of the design process developed into a concept of
'*the* design method' (rather than the looser concept of 'design methods')
at a conference in Birmingham in 1965 (Gregory, 1966). There was a
conscious intention on the part of the conference organizers "to establish
a common basis of agreement about the nature of 'the design method',
using this phrase in the same way as the 'scientific method'". However,
no agreed view, nor even a consensus, on the 'the design method' seems
to emerge from the thirty-five papers of the published proceedings,
despite the fact that almost all deal solely with engineering design.

2.1.2 Design method in architecture
There was nevertheless considerable enthusiasm for 'design method in
architecture' (Broadbent, 1966) at this time, particularly as an aid to the
learning of design skills in the schools of architecture. Broadbent claimed
that "there is evidence already that, in certain schools of architecture,
systematic design can not only structure the teacher's and student's tasks,
but that it will also improve standards of design... This suggests that
architectural education has made a valuable contribution which in the long
run will inevitably raise standards in practice".

This enthusiasm carried through a conference/course on The Teaching of
Design—Design Method in Architecture held at Ulm in 1966, and a
conference on Design Methods in Architecture (Broadbent and Ward,
1969) held at Portsmouth in 1967. Yet very soon there was a distinct
waning of enthusiasm. In 1968 the same author who had claimed two
years earlier that there was "evidence" that systematic design would
"improve standards of design" and was a "valuable contribution", now
suggested that these same systematic design processes "tend to look too
formal, too systematized, too cut and dried" (Broadbent, 1968). Indeed,
within but two years it seemed that "design method has not fared too well".

Despite this apparent change in the evidence of the success of systematic
design, conferences on essentially that topic continued to flourish; except
now the conferences were almost exclusively concerned with architecture
or environmental design and were held in the United States. There was a

conference on 'emerging methods' at MIT in 1968 (Moore, 1970), and there have been annual 'environmental design research' conferences in the United States since 1969. A conference on The Application of Systematic Methods to Designing was held in Berkeley, California, in 1975. Meanwhile, a more broadly ranging conference on The Design Activity had been held in London in 1973, and the first textbook of design methods had been published (Jones, 1970).

Perhaps the most significant feature of the conferences from 1968 onwards was the number of papers on computer-aided design. This work had its roots in the earlier approaches to systematic design, but seemed to develop on a pragmatic basis despite the doubts and waverings of the erstwhile protagonists of 'design method'. In fact computer-aided design became a major subject in its own right, with a vast series of conferences and publications in both Europe and the United States. This development will be considered in more detail later.

2.2 The design process

It would perhaps have been more fruitful for the systematic designers to have looked at the design process, rather than to have searched for a design method. Although Broadbent (1968) considered that "design method has not fared too well", he still maintained that fields such as operational research "have a great deal to offer the designer; they are, in fact, crucial to the development of new design methods—*provided that they can be slotted into a sequence determined by the needs of architecture itself*" (my emphasis). It seems doubtful whether the "needs of architecture itself" could ever be established, although the needs of the architect perhaps could be. Broadbent implies that, if there were a greater understanding of the process used by designers, aids to that process (design methods, computer aids, etc) could reliably be developed. This is a much more pragmatic approach to the evolution of the design process, which avoids the need to develop first a grand theory of design method.

2.2.1 Design research

Unfortunately very little research on the design process has been conducted. Most of the contributions to the various conferences have been based on the authors' speculations on the nature of the design process, rather than on reliable research.

Levin (1966a; 1966b) is one of the few people to have attempted systematically to observe designers (town planners) at work. He suggested that the design process is a learning process—the designer explores, by a trial-and-error process, the general problem as given, and thus gradually exposes the details of the problem. "It seems that often it is only by actually designing that a designer will become aware of problems such as the conflict of two user requirements" (Levin, 1966a).

The design process is different from other learning processes, however, in that there is no defined body of knowledge, which the designer could be helped towards learning or discovering. Levin (1966b) likened the design situation to certain kinds of mathematical riddle "in which there always seems to be insufficient information to give an answer. Then you remember that you have another bit of information, namely that the problem is to be solvable, and this is the extra information that you need. Likewise, the designer knows (consciously or unconsciously) that some ingredient must be added to the information that he already has in order that he may arrive at an unique solution". The designer uses his powers of conjecture and original thought to look for this extra ingredient, which is usually an 'ordering principle'—geometric patterns, for example.

Levin's practical analysis of the design process is in fact reflected in the statements of some of the design theorists. Jones (1966) for example has said that designing should not solely be equated with problem solving but also with 'problem finding'. Similarly Asimow (1962) wrote: "The designer is presented not with a problem but with a problem situation, (and) it is out of this milieu of perplexity that clear definitions of the relevant problems must be drawn".

2.2.2 Cyclical structures

In this problem situation Levin found 'trees' of decision areas, although in some cases the branches of the trees in fact form loops of interdependent decision areas—that is, A cannot be decided before B, B cannot be decided before C, and C cannot be decided before A. For example, if the town planner has to locate public open space P, industry I, and housing H within a designated area, he might start, Levin suggests, by locating P first, since that decision is where he prefers to allow himself most freedom of choice (for example so as to be able to select the most attractive areas). He might then locate I, again on the basis of preferred sites. In theory these two decisions have effectively also decided the location of H—in the areas that remain. However, in practice the remaining areas will not necessarily all be suitable or adequate for the housing that has to be provided, and the planner has to reconsider his decisions on P and then I again. Thus the decision areas P, I, and H are connected in a loop that the planner could circle virtually endlessly. Most designers will be familiar with this situation, and it is in this situation that the 'extra ingredient' has to be generated by the designer in order to resolve the problem.

Luckman (1967) reached a similar conclusion on the interdependent nature of decisionmaking in design from a study of the architectural design process. This study was part of a Building Communication Research Project carried out jointly by the Tavistock Institute of Human Relations and the Institute for Operational Research. Luckman went on to devise a method for the Analysis of Interconnected Decision Areas (AIDA), which he offered as a contribution to systematic design from operational research.

The use of AIDA was demonstrated by Luckman with respect to a case study from the joint research project. This case study was the design of a house. The researchers observed that the design team "were attempting to make their decisions sequentially, when in fact almost every decision was affected both by those that had gone and those that were yet to come". Luckman showed the pattern of interdependent decision areas in the form of a decision graph (figure 2.2).

The links in the decision graph indicate in each case that some of the options in the linked decision areas are mutually constraining. For example, in the particular circumstances of the case study, it would not have been possible to have the direction of span of the first floor joists between the side crosswalls, without having load-bearing core partitions on the ground floor (because the span presumably would have been too great without the intermediate support of the partitions).

AIDA provided a fairly simple means of systematically devising and listing all the combinations of compatible options for the complete set of decision areas. By applying some criterion such as cost, an optimum option set can be identified. (It is interesting, though, that in this example Luckman acknowledges that the minimum-cost solution derived by AIDA was in fact the same solution that the design team had arrived at independently.)

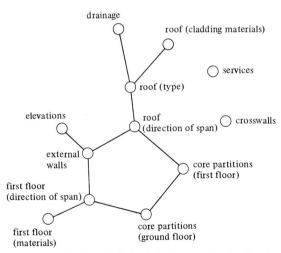

Figure 2.2. Luckman's (1967) decision graph for the design of a house.

2.2.3 Hierarchical structures

Comparable studies of designers in other areas have not, however, found quite the same patterns of decisionmaking in the design process. Marples (1960) made a study of engineering designers and found decision 'trees', as had Levin with town planners, but not the cyclical decision loops that were evident in both studies of environmental designers. Marples found a distinct hierarchy of decision areas; once the designers had made a decision at one level, it led to a clear set of options at a lower level, and so on. Thus Marples found a linear design process in operation.

Gregory (1964) also found a virtually linear process in a case study taken from chemical engineering design, although there were some significant recycling loops evident in the process (figure 2.3). Gregory reports, though, that these loops were broken by making particular decisions within single decision areas that were causing the recycling, not by resolving

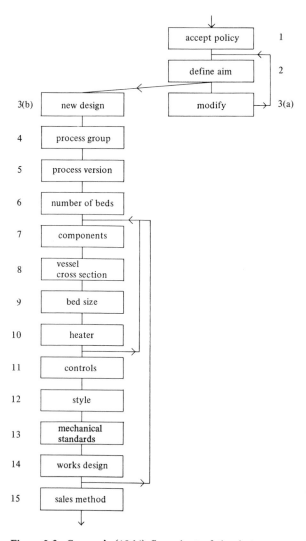

Figure 2.3. Gregory's (1964) flow chart of the design process in a particular chemical engineering design problem.

a set of interconnected decisions in concert. Thus Gregory's analysis of the design process is similar to some of the theoretical 'design method' structures, such as that of Archer (1965).

2.2.4 Two-dimensional structures

These theoretical linear structures have often been criticized for their 'one-dimensional' approach to the design process. Markus (1967), amongst others, has suggested that the design process is at least two-dimensional: it contains a 'vertical' structure of sequential design stages, and a 'horizontal' structure of iterative and cyclical design procedures. The 'vertical' structure regulates the development of a design (for example from outline to detail proposals) and is embodied in recommended structures for engineering design (Asimow, 1962), industrial design (Archer, 1965), and architectural design (RIBA, 1967). See table 2.2 for a comparative listing of these recommended structures. The table indicates that there are significant parallels between many stages of 'systematic design' in all three professions, but that there also appear to be some differences between the three design processes. Thus there is only limited agreement on a common 'design process'.

The 'horizontal' structure of the design process appears within most of the 'vertical' stages and is usually represented as some derivative of the original three-part 'process', analysis–synthesis–evaluation (figure 2.4).

This two-dimensional structure for the design process probably represents a consensus compromise between what the process actually *is* and what it *should be*. After all, few of the contributions to the debate on systematic design have been concerned merely with reporting on the status quo in design; they have generally been a significant part of the pressures for change and evolution in the design process.

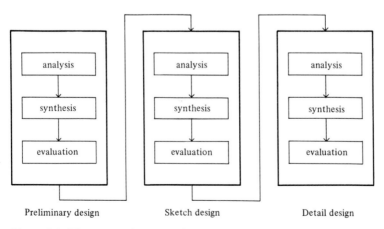

Figure 2.4. The commonly accepted two-dimensional model of the design process.

B

Table 2.2. A comparison of recommended structures of the design process for architecture, industrial design, and engineering design.

Architecture (RIBA, 1967)	Industrial design (Archer, 1965)	Engineering design (Asimow, 1962)
		Primitive need
A. Inception	0. Preliminaries receive and evaluate enquiry	1. Feasibility demonstrate the validity of the original need; explore the design problem engendered by the need; conceive a number of plausible solutions to the problem
B. Feasibility provide the client with an appraisal and recommendation; carry out studies of user requirements, site conditions, planning, design, cost, etc	1. Briefing receive instructions; define goals; define constraints	
	2. Programming establish crucial issues; propose a course of action	
	3. Data collection collect, classify, and store data	
C. Outline proposals determine general approach to layout, design, and construction; develop the brief further; carry out studies on user requirements, technical problems, planning, design, and costs	4. Analysis identify subproblems; prepare performance (or design) specification; reappraise proposed programme and estimate	2. Preliminary design establish which alternative is the best design concept; conduct order-of-magnitude analyses; establish range within which major design parameters must be controlled; investigate tolerances and characteristics of major components and materials
	5. Synthesis prepare outline design proposals	
D. Scheme design final development of the brief; full design of the project by architect; preliminary design by engineers; preparation of cost plan and full explanatory report	6. Development develop prototype design(s); prepare and execute validation studies	

3. Detailed design
   furnish the engineering description of a tested and producible design

4. Planning for production
   detailed planning of the manufacturing processes

5. Planning for distribution
   plan an effective and flexible system of distribution of the designed product

6. Planning for consumption
   incorporate in the design adequate service features; provide a rational basis for product improvement and redesign

7. Planning for retirement
   plan for the disposal of the obsolete product

7. Communication
   prepare manufacturing documentation

8. Winding-up
   wind-up project; close records

E. Detail design
   full design of every part and component of the building; complete cost checking of designs

F. Production information
   preparation of final production information—that is, drawings, schedules, and specifications

G. Bills of Quantities

H. Tender action

J. Project planning

K. Operations on site

L. Completion

M. Feedback
   Analysis of job records; inspections of completed building; studies of building in use

2.3 The development of computer aids

Computer aids to design have been an integral part of the general systematic design movement since its inception. Alexander's (1963) paper to the 1962 conference, for example, presented his method, which relied on the use of a computer, for rationally determining the physical components of a city. (At least in principle it was concerned with cities; in practice, Alexander used as an example a 'city in miniature'—an Indian village.)

Alexander explained that his method was "based on non-numerical mathematics. It arises largely from the use of graphs (topological 1-complexes) to represent systems of interacting functions. Since the application of the method demands rather a lot of computation and manipulation, I have used the IBM 7090 computer to carry it out". The reference to the amount of computation and manipulation that was required was a typical justification for the use of computers at that time. That is, the computer was seen to be able to offer new possibilities that had previously been out of the reach of the computational abilities of human beings. This attitude towards the uses of computers probably stemmed from their wartime 'number-crunching' origins, and from the fact that in 1962 they were still massive, expensive machines; still regarded, in other words, as 'giant brains'. Since that time attitudes towards computers have changed radically as they have become smaller, cheaper, and much more accessible, and as they have been used more in communication and control functions—for example in banking, transport, education—rather than as remote 'brains'.

As the computer's role evolved and changed so fundamentally throughout the nineteen-sixties, computer-aided design (CAD) became the cuckoo in the systematic design nest. By the time of the 1968 conference at MIT (Moore, 1970) fifty percent of the papers were directly concerned with the use of computer aids in design. Now systematic design is virtually regarded as synonymous with computer-aided design. Many design researchers would regard computer-aided design methods as the truest form of systematic methods almost by definition, since only procedures that are genuinely systematic can be described in machine form.

The rapid and extensive development of computer-aided design methods was undoubtedly promoted by the rapid increase in accessibility of computers which happened in the mid-sixties. This accessibility was occasioned by developments in both hardware (cheaper, smaller computers, remote terminals, etc) and software (English language programming, multiaccess systems, etc), so that by about 1967 access to a computer could be had quite easily at any conventional telephone location. Thus in the space of a few years people no longer talked of computers in terms of the concept of 'giant brains', but of the concept of 'the computer in the home'.

At about the same time, rapid developments taking place in architecture considerably enhanced the relevance of the computer as an aid to architectural design. These developments were in the promotion and relatively widespread adoption of system building techniques—the use of standardized, prefabricated building components. The use of these techniques particularly suited computer-aided design methods because they meant that the architect was then dealing with a finite range of components whose attributes (dimensions, costs, materials, strengths, etc) were known.

This made life a lot easier for the computer programmers, who could now establish dimensional grids, catalogues of components, etc that a computer could readily handle. Instead of the virtually infinite freedom of design in traditional building, the architect working with system building was constrained within a system boundary which could also be managed by the machine. This strong link between computer-aided design and system building remains effective, and most of the comprehensive CAD systems under development or in application are based on particular building systems.

The following brief review of three typical comprehensive CAD systems —CEDAR, Harness, and West Sussex—indicates the general nature of current developments in this field.

2.3.1 The CEDAR system

One such example of a CAD system based on a building system is the CEDAR (Computer-aided Environmental Design Analysis and Realisation) system under development in the Property Services Agency of the Department of the Environment (DoE). This system is intended to be implemented in the DoE architectural design offices for the design of certain buildings using the SEAC building system. Chalmers (1972) explains the relevance of SEAC thus: "SEAC have developed a metric mark of their building system using predefined components for the major elements of the building assembled together according to dimensional and jointing rules which can be readily analysed into procedures. In this way individually designed details are replaced in a SEAC building by references to standard drawings and specifications. This results in a great reduction of the data required to describe a project and the SEAC system provides a well-defined vehicle for development of a CAD system".

The aims and procedure of the CEDAR system were outlined by Chalmers thus: "The system proposed would carry information about the project being designed in computer files. The design would be developed by the designer working through terminal equipment linked to the central computer. The facilities the initial system would offer the designer would include interactive programs for building up detailed designs, analysis and automatic detailing of designs where permitted by the SEAC system and the output of information for the contractor and component manufacturers in the form of drawings, schedules and computer storage media... Benefits would come from the automation of information handling in the design process and more accurate designs leading to lower building costs".

2.3.2 The Harness system

Standardization in architectural design has been taken much further than prefabricated construction components by the Department of Health and Social Security (DHSS), in hospital design. DHSS hospital planners have developed the Harness system, which incorporates predesigned, standard, whole departments (Radford, 1974). The architectural design task for a new hospital is thereby limited to arranging these department building blocks along a circulation spine (the 'Harness'). This rather elementary design function is, of course, extremely computer-compatible.

One significant feature of the Harness system that endears it to the computer programmers is, as Meager (1972) rather obliquely puts it, "the number of things which the designer does not have to watch out for". Putting it more directly, one might perhaps say that there is not very much for the designer actually to do. This interpretation is strengthened by a knowledge of the second computer-compatible feature identified by Meager, which is that "the building packages which the designer handles in development planning are really quite large—up to say $£\frac{1}{2}$-million worth of building. So the *number* of packages that have to be arranged to form a development plan are correspondingly small—about thirty for a complete hospital".

Meager notes that these stringent variety-reducing features of the Harness system "made the computer-aided assembly of whole hospitals, and their evaluation, accessible for the first time. The majority of the constraints, problems of compatibility and the sheer size of computation which bedevil most attempts at computer-aided building *design*, were by-passed" (his emphasis).

Two sets of computer programs have been developed for use with the Harness system. One set accepts the designer's proposed Harness layout, with its assembly of departments, and evaluates this proposal in terms of circulation efficiency, capital cost, heat loss, and site usage. When the designer has an evaluation he is satisfied with (perhaps after modification of the original proposal), the computer can help to locate lifts and other components of the 'Harness zone' (circulation spine), evaluate daylighting levels, and eventually produce production documents. A second set of design programs, however, can be used to assemble automatically the required hospital departments around the Harness zone, with circulation efficiency as the criterion for assembly. The configuration of the zone appears to be the only creative input from the designer required at this level of design automation. Meager does point out, though, that "the intention of this second set of programs is to encourage the designer to move swiftly through a number of radically different design concepts. Here an attempt has been made to help the designer overcome the very common syndrome of fixation with his early ideas".

2.3.3 The West Sussex system

Of course, not all applications of computer-aided design are linked so closely with such extreme forms of standardization. In fact most research work has been concerned with discrete applications programs, rather than with integrated computer/building systems. Even integrated systems do not have to have a specific building system as a prerequisite. Instead a more ad hoc 'library catalogue' of building components can be used, as was the case with the pioneering computer-aided system of the West Sussex County Architect's Department (Ray-Jones, 1968; Paterson, 1974).

Paterson outlined the operation of the West Sussex system up to the scheme-design stage as follows:

"The site is inspected and surveyed, and the results of this investigation are fed into the computer, which on the one hand is able to hold this information for future design use, and on the other, produce via a digital plotter, a site survey plan which gives not only the levels, but also information on views or anything else the designer may conceivably need. Whilst this is proceeding, a brief is being developed... By collecting information on human requirements of all ages and the activities and equipment which are associated with them, a brief based on sortations of priorities and correlations of requirements can quickly be produced. The idea of this brief is based on the view that, say a doctor, teacher or executive of the same age will probably have the same needs and characteristics when, say, writing at a desk. Therefore, simple files can cover a large briefing need because the files are related to basic activities.

"The computer is able to make sortations (which one suspects is the way an architect works) of the most economic circulation routes, or the best relationship of one person to another, or those requiring daylight, or those not requiring daylight, etc. The designer can then look at these sortations and make a mix, or choose one as he desires. By feeding in geographic data the relationship of this information to local need can be considered.

"At this stage the designer is able, with the information available, to begin to mould his brief into the shape of a possible building. He is at present able to go to the screen of the light-pen display unit and by indicating the type of project that he is developing, that is, school, health centre, etc, and the appropriate exposure area, he can start to develop his sketch design.

"When he has indicated the general shape and requirements of the building he has in mind, he is able to check his scheme for approximate cost, heat loss and air change, and therefore the running costs of the building, and to check on daylight factors, if required. He has the opportunity of testing other solutions at this stage so that he can be sure of starting his design on the right basis".

2.3.4 Computer graphics

Graphical computer input/output devices, such as the plotter, and the light pen and display screen referred to by Paterson, have significantly widened the range of potential computer applications in architectural design. Plotters can rapidly produce a variety of different types of drawings from a basic set of data and have obvious applications in the preparation of the different sets of drawings that are required by architect, quantity surveyor, builder, subcontractors, etc, in a building project. Conversely a digitizer can be used to input information (locations, dimensions, etc) to the computer directly from existing drawings. The light pen can be used for more interactive communication between designer and computer, through the medium of a cathode-ray-tube (CRT) display.

Design seems inherently a visual process, and, as a rule, certainly relies on the use of drawings both as a design aid and as a communication medium. Computer graphics, however, were originally too expensive for general application, since they demanded a large dedicated computer capacity simply to keep the CRT display device constantly 'refreshed', that is continually regenerated in the same manner as the normal television picture. In the later 1960s this situation was changed by the development of direct-view storage tubes which do not require constant refreshing, although they do not possess the same inherent capability for graphical manipulation as does the cathode-ray tube. Many current computer applications to architectural design now rely on the use of these storage tubes. (See, for example, the illustrations of the SPACES system in the next chapter.)

3

Computer-aided design

3.1 Computer analysis

Many hundreds of computer programs dealing with aspects of architectural design have been written in addition to the more comprehensive and integrated computer-aided design systems such as CEDAR, Harness, and the West Sussex examples. The complete analysis–synthesis–evaluation design spectrum is now covered by, not to say littered with, a variety of computer aids.

At the analysis end of the spectrum Alexander's (1963) pioneering example has already been mentioned. Alexander's method was conceived in his concern to find a way of determining "the right physical components of a physical structure" that would be free of the preconceptions lodged in the designer's mind of the *conventional* components of, say, a city. Thus "the habit of mind which says that the city's component building blocks are houses, streets, parks and offices, is so strong that we take the components for granted: what we call design, consists of playing variations on the kinds of city you can get by arranging and rearranging these components. But this never leads to a new structure for the city... The fundamental change which the structure undergoes at the hands of a great designer, who is able to redistribute its functions altogether, cannot take place if its components stay the same".

3.1.1 Hierarchical trees

To achieve this radical, unpreconceived structuring of a design problem, Alexander's method of hierarchical trees begins by having the designer prepare an exhaustive list of all the requirements that might affect the physical structure of the design. This list will naturally be rather long in anything other than a trivial problem. Alexander lists 141 such requirements in his example of an Indian village of 600 inhabitants, and these requirements range over what seems to be every conceivable feature of village life, such as:

7. Cattle treated as sacred, and vegetarian attitude.
18. Need to divide land among sons and successive generations.
24. Place for village events—dancing, plays, singing, wrestling.
67. Drinking water to be good, sweet.
78. Shade for sitting and walking.
92. House has to be cleaned, washed, drained.

These components will form the basis of a rational structure for the new village; a structure composed as a hierarchical 'tree' of subsystems. The lowest level of subsystems is found by grouping the requirements in independent sets (or sets that are as independent of each other as possible), and it is this partitioning of the requirements that demands the use of a computer.

B*

Each requirement is first considered in relationship to every other requirement, to see if the pair interact with each other (for example, requirement 67 interacts with requirement 92). This information is used in the computer program to partition the requirements into groups that are, ideally, very densely connected internally but as far as possible independent of any other group. These groups are thus a rational sub-division of the total problem, which may offer a completely new interpretation of the structure of the village. The structure is built up by devising physical components to satisfy the separate groups of requirements and by gradually combining these components into an overall design for the village.

A further example of the method was demonstrated by Chermayeff and Alexander (1963). This example was concerned with the relationship of public space in housing layouts, for which thirty-three requirements were listed.

The computer program (HIDECS) for this method of hierarchical decomposition of problem elements was developed by Alexander and Manheim (1962). The central idea of Alexander's method has proved to be a popular one (although it was subsequently virtually revoked by Alexander, 1966), and considerable work has been conducted on similar programs based on this idea—that design problems can be analyzed as clusters of interconnected elements to be hierarchically combined.

3.1.2 CLUSTER

Milne (1970) suggests that his computer program CLUSTER can be considered as a second generation descendant of earlier programs such as HIDECS. CLUSTER accepts as input the basic information of a list of requirements together with an interaction matrix giving their paired relationships. The program then identifies all the 'simplexes' of three or more elements (where a simplex is a set of elements, each of which interacts with all others) and prints out the list of simplexes. It then goes on to compose a hierarchical problem structure tree by combining the most 'coherent' (a measure of interconnectivity) pairs of simplexes into new problem subsets, combining the most coherent subsets thus formed, etc, until one final set remains.

Milne illustrates the use of CLUSTER with an example of the design of a study carrel. Eighteen basic requirements were identified in this problem:
1. Student likes to lean on work surface.
2. Student likes to spread out materials within reach and view.
3. Reorganization of materials is an undesirable disruption of study.
4. Student likes to know his materials are secure in his absence.
5. Student likes adequate book storage within reach and view.
6. Student likes a place to accumulate small items.
7. Student likes organized storage of loose-leaf materials.
8. Study process generates waste.

9. Bulk storage is needed for special study equipment.
10. Student sometimes uses a typewriter.
11. A variety of comfortable positions is necessary for writing, typing, relaxed reading.
12. Student likes to come and go at will.
13. Student likes a controlled visual contact with an interesting external environment.
14. Student likes the option of visual privacy.
15. Personal control of auditory environment is essential.
16. Student would like to modify temperature and air movement.
17. Feeling of confinement is undesirable.
18. Student should have the option of controlling illumination.

Eighteen simplex groups were found from this list by the CLUSTER program: for example, requirements 3, 4, 5, 6, 7 formed one simplex; 3, 4, 12, 14 formed another; and so on. The way these groups were then coupled hierarchically by CLUSTER is shown in figure 3.1. The program

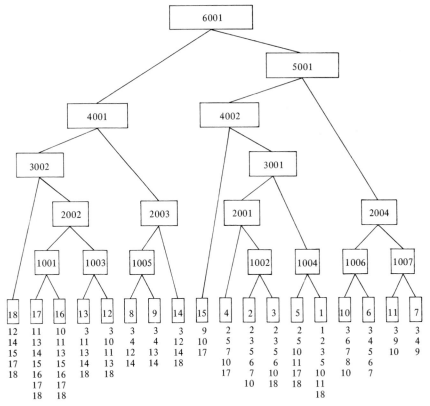

Figure 3.1. The hierarchical semilattice structure of the study-carrel problem, as composed by the CLUSTER program. (Source: Milne, 1970).

also prints out lists of all the 'conjunctive elements' (mutual elements in the lower groups) at each combination point; for example the subset labelled 1001 contains the conjunctive elements 11, 13, 15, 16, 17, 18. Because of the overlap of conjunctive elements, Milne claims that the recomposition structure is a 'semilattice' (see Alexander, 1966) rather than a 'tree'.

Milne considers that "these conjunctive elements give the designer a valuable clue as to the main organizing principle that binds the sub-problems together." He suggests that the designer could scan the recomposition structure to find the most meaningful level of problem. "If he can solve this problem, he need only check the solution against every subproblem below this point, and he can then begin to combine this solution with the appropriate clusters above this point. This is a great time-saver because it means that the designer will not have to solve all the first level subproblems but can concentrate on only the most meaningful clusters, many of which will be found higher up the recomposition structure."

3.1.3 MDS

An alternative technique for clustering problem elements, based on multi-dimensional scaling (MDS), has been reviewed by Kernohan et al. (1971). MDS, which was borrowed from the behavioural sciences, is a technique for representing proximity relationships; that is, it converts numerical information about a set of elements into a spatial configuration. It takes an input of a relationship matrix which is similar to that used in HIDECS and CLUSTER except that the relationships between pairs of problem elements can be expressed in varying magnitudes, rather than just 1 or 0. Thus the *relative strengths* of the relationships can be considered, a facility that may be useful for some kinds of architectural design problems (for example in assessing the way different elements of accommodation would 'naturally' cluster in relative locations).

MDS can provide an output in multidimensional 'space', but it is doubtful if anything other than two-dimensional or three-dimensional space would be meaningful in architecture. A two-dimensional output provides a visual indication of the way in which the problem elements tend to cluster in groups on the basis of the relative strengths of their interrelationships. This visual planning aid is an obvious benefit in architectural design, in comparison with the lengthy tabulations produced by programs such as CLUSTER.

3.1.4 AIDA

The AIDA method (Luckman, 1967) of analyzing design problems into compatible option sets has already been mentioned (chapter 2). This method assumes that a number of decision areas can be identified, each of which contains a number of possible options, and that some of these options are mutually incompatible across decision areas. In many cases this will mean that the problem can be approached only as a set of elements which all interact at one level—that is, neither hierarchical decomposition nor sequential decisionmaking is possible. For these cases AIDA offers a computer program that lists all the sets of compatible options, so that the designer is presented with a clear choice of the possible sets of simultaneous decisions.

The computer programs written for design analysis therefore reflect the different views (reviewed in chapter 2) that are held of the structure of design problems. That is, the structure is seen as either hierarchical (whether in tree or semilattice form) or cyclical.

3.2 Computer synthesis

Using the computer as a more direct aid in the synthesis stage of design problems, or actually as a means of automatically generating design solutions, has fascinated most research workers in computer-aided architectural design. In general this fascination has centred on the room-layout or space-allocation problem, which is of course a central architectural design problem. Broadbent (1973) estimates that "over one quarter of all published programs, not to mention academic papers about computing, are concerned with space allocation and circulation". As evidence he tabulates the numbers of computer programs for different aspects of architectural work that were included in major British and American listings of 1969–1970. Of the 213 programs listed, 58 are in the category 'Space allocation and circulation in buildings'. Table 3.1, however, based on a more recent British survey, suggests that this concern for 'schematic design' is a preoccupation of research, not practice. At least one whole book (Eastman, 1975) has been devoted to the subject of spatial synthesis in CAD.

Most of the space-allocation programs are concerned with generating a solution (that is, a complete layout or configuration of the spaces to be allocated in the overall problem) by optimizing on a selected performance criterion (or occasionally a set of performance criteria). Usually the performance criterion chosen is the amount of user circulation between rooms (journeys x distances) that any given plan would entail. That is, it is assumed that rooms that have a lot of traffic between them, because of the nature of the normal activities that go on in the building, should ideally be only a short distance apart. Thus an optimum solution would be one in which the overall figure for journeys x distances is minimized.

An early example of this approach to architectural design was that of Moseley (1963), who used linear programming techniques to optimize the circulation problem. Whitehead and Eldars (1964; 1965) produced one of the first examples of a computer program that would automatically generate a room layout.

Table 3.1. The numbers of computer applications reported to be in use by research groups, government design offices, and private design practices (the latter includes other building-team participants besides architects), in a survey by Applied Research of Cambridge (1973). The table shows clearly the different interests and emphases of the different bodies.

Applications		Research groups	Government design offices	Private design practices
Site and land-use studies				
Site mapping		2	5	2
Cut and fill		0	3	0
Site layout		3	4	1
Housing mix		0	2	1
Road layout		1	2	0
Land-use costs		4	5	1
	Total	10	21	5
Brief analysis				
Activity data		1	5	2
Accommodation schedules		3	3	2
Cluster diagrams		1	1	1
	Total	5	9	5
Schematic design				
Circulation		4	1	1
Single-storey layouts		6	2	0
Multi-storey layouts		4	2	1
Drainage layouts		2	5	0
	Total	16	10	2
Scheme and performance evaluation				
Heat gain		6	3	1
Heat loss		7	3	3
Daylighting		10	4	1
Artificial lighting		1	2	1
Sound transmission		5	0	1
Sound reverberation		0	0	1
Natural ventilation		3	3	0
Artificial ventilation		1	1	0
Air-conditioning loads		2	2	1
Lift simulation		1	2	0
Wind loading		1	2	1
	Total	37	22	10
Detail design				
Plant sizing		2	2	1
Pipe sizing		2	2	1
Structural sizing		0	5	3
Services design		0	2	1
Architectural details		4	4	0
	Total	8	15	6

Table 3.1 (continued).

Applications		Research groups	Government design offices	Private design practices
Costing				
Job-cost models		6	5	4
Preambles		0	3	2
Bill of quantities		4	6	8
Priced-bill analysis		0	1	1
Resources allocation		1	0	6
Specifications		0	1	1
	Total	11	16	22
Production information				
General assembly drawings		0	4	1
Reinforced concrete details		0	2	1
Assembly drawings		2	3	1
Component schedules		2	4	7
Location analysis		1	4	5
	Total	5	17	15
Project control				
Network analysis		1	1	0
Precedence diagram		0	1	0
Project cost control		1	1	4
	Total	2	3	4
In-house administration				
Job costing		0	2	4
Time and payroll		0	2	3
Invoicing		0	1	1
	Total	0	5	8

3.2.1 The Whitehead and Eldars program

As with the hierarchical decomposition and clustering type of analysis programs, the input to the Whitehead and Eldars program (and all such room-layout programs) is a matrix covering all the interactions (journeys in this case) between all possible pairs of rooms to be accommodated. These interactions are initially stated in terms of the number of journeys made between each pair of rooms over some representative time period (say, one day). The data for this can be recorded from observation and monitoring of the journeys made in an existing building of the type that is being designed. Weightings can then be given to different types of users, if desired, to produce a final set of modified data which now reflects the 'strength' of the interaction between each pair of rooms. For example in the hospital design used as a demonstration by Whitehead and Eldars the surgeons' journeys were given a considerably higher weighting than those of the nurses.

The Whitehead and Eldars program then searches the matrix to identify the room with the highest level of interaction with all other rooms and places that room in the centre of a predetermined planning grid. It then identifies the room with the highest level of interaction with this first room, and places the second room adjacent to the first. The third room to be placed is that having the highest level of interaction with the first and second rooms combined, and remaining rooms are selected in a similar way as the program proceeds. To place these subsequent rooms (beyond the second) the program makes trial placings of each room around the edges of the nest of rooms that have already been placed, and calculates the 'cost' of each of these trial placings. The 'cost' is the sum of the number of journeys × the distance between the room being placed and all previously placed rooms. The least-cost position is eventually chosen, and the program continues to build up a plan for the building in this way.

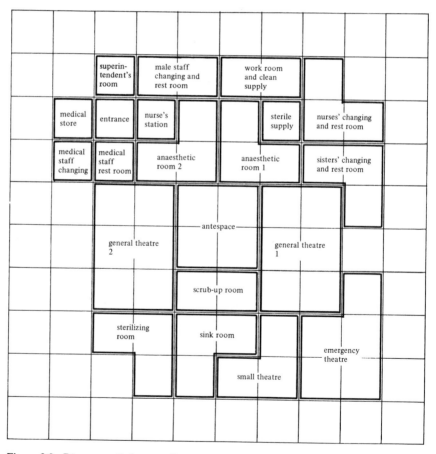

Figure 3.2. Diagrammatic layout of an operating theatre suite derived from the Whitehead and Eldars (1964; 1965) room-layout computer program.

Some relatively minor sophistications are incorporated into the program —for example, different room sizes can be dealt with by making all rooms a multiple of a standard modular plan area—but the program essentially produces a rather crude version of a building plan (figure 3.2). This crude plan still requires some planning ingenuity to convert it into a realistic plan. Nevertheless the Whitehead and Eldars program (and the many similar versions) must be regarded as a significant aid to a designer who is concerned to achieve a 'rational' synthesis.

It should perhaps be noted that the locational programs such as that of Whitehead and Eldars do not necessarily generate a truly optimum solution—their aim is only to get near the optimum. This lack of optimality is inevitable, since there is no certain (that is algorithmic) means of finding the true optimum to problems of such size and complexity as are normal in architectural design.

3.2.2 Minimum house plans

In very constrained architectural problems (such as house design), however, it may be possible to consider generating solutions that are of truly minimal 'cost' (however that criterion may be measured). The AIDA example of Luckman (1967) generated the minimum-cost solution to the particular house design problem being considered. Another approach to automatically generating minimum-cost (in this case, construction cost) house designs that fit given constraints of dimensions, areas, and adjacencies has been developed by Mitchell (1974).

Mitchell's method is based on the use of a 'catalogue' of all the basic geometric configurations that are possible for a small number (up to approximately seven) of rectangles. This catalogue is established and stored in the computer. Then, given the adjacency requirements of rooms in any particular design problem, the computer program identifies those basic configurations that satisfy these requirements. Given also the constraints on dimensions that apply to each of the rooms in the problem, the program will adjust the suitable basic configurations of rectangles into plan forms that meet these constraints. Finally the program determines the optimum, minimum-cost plan from the set of feasible alternatives.

Steadman (1970) has also proposed a means for automatically generating minimum-standard house plans subject to similar adjacency, dimensional, etc constraints. This method draws on the theory of graphs and a 'curious analogy' from the physics of electrical networks, by which Kirchoff's Laws of electrical flow are applied to relationships between the dimensions and shapes of rectangles packed together as in an architectural plan. Permutational methods are also applied, so as to identify every possible solution that meets the given constraints.

Recent developments in this work to establish all conceivable solutions to modest floor-plan problems (such as house plans) are reported by Mitchell et al (1976).

3.2.3 STUNI

An attempt at computer synthesis of more complex plans than any of
the above programs consider is contained in the program of Willoughby
et al (1970). The program is known as 'STUNI', from its original
development in connection with a design for Stirling University, and is
applicable to design problems, such as that of a university campus, in
which a variety of departments have to be located on a relatively large site.
In a university these departments or 'activity units' would be the School of
Engineering, the Arts Faculty, the Library, student residences, and so on.

The input data for STUNI consists of a relationship matrix similar to
that used by Whitehead and Eldars. It gives the relationship values for
each pair of departments, plus values of 'internal' relationships for the
elements within each department. Each department is therefore assumed
to consist of a number of elements, all of a standard plan area. In
addition the site is divided into a regular grid of the same standard
dimensions (say 1000 m² squares), and each site grid location thus
established is given a desirability value (perhaps based on its aspect, or
load-bearing capacity, etc). The STUNI program takes these location
desirability values into consideration in planning the arrangement of

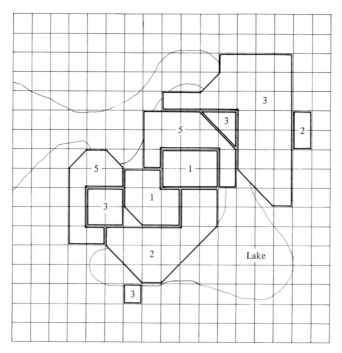

Figure 3.3. A 'zoning diagram' site layout for a university, derived from the STUNI
program. The figure given for each block indicates its storey height. (Source:
Willoughby et al, 1970).

departments on the site. These desirability values can be different for each different department.

The selection and placing of the elements of each activity unit is somewhat similar to that already described for the Whitehead and Eldars program, except that site values are now also added into the computation for the 'cost' of each possible location of each new element. There are also the 'internal' (high value) relationships between elements, as well as their 'external' relationships to elements in other activity units, to be taken into account. STUNI also offers the designer the choice of locating the first activity unit on the site (or any other prepositioning of units) or of leaving this to the program for a completely automatic solution.

STUNI therefore incorporates some significant improvements over the Whitehead and Eldars program. It recognizes, and accommodates, a much greater problem complexity; it allows some interaction between the designer and the program; and it will also produce multistorey solutions. The 'zoning diagram' produced by the authors from their application of the program to the Stirling University design problem is shown in figure 3.3.

3.2.4 BAID

The site-layout problem has also been approached in an interesting way by Auger (1972) with respect to housing layouts. Auger's BAID (Basic Architectural Investigation and Design) program generates site layouts in which units are placed at random by the computer, subject to certain constraints being satisfied. For example a randomly chosen location would be rejected if it did not fulfil requirements of daylight, sunlight, and privacy. Thus each unit located on the site would be checked by the program to ensure that it had "a minimum of 1% of the sky visible at every point on each window face, this percentage being viewed through a standard aperture which ensures adequate light at the back of each room. It also has a minimum of two hours of sunlight for ten months of the year falling on the full width of one window face, and no window face is closer than $18 \cdot 3$ m (70 ft) to any directly opposing window face".

Many site layouts can be generated by this program—it does not attempt to search for an 'optimum'. Each layout generated is likely to be different from the one before, as the layout is determined by random selection of locations which are then checked to ensure that the relevant criteria are fulfilled. Whether or not any particular possible location is included in a layout will therefore depend on the sequence of random numbers generated by the computer, and the existing configuration of the site layout at the time that that location's number came up.

Auger obviously intends that these random layouts should be used by the designer as a stimulus and guide, rather than that they should be accepted directly as produced by the computer. He illustrates three random layouts produced for the same site, and then his own layout, which was produced "after a few minutes' study of the three layouts".

The designer can therefore introduce considerations that were not programmed into the computer. Auger states that "the object of producing the random generated layouts is to stimulate the designer's imagination, give him a sense of scale for the site, and provide him with possible ideas for groupings, etc". When the designer has produced his own version of a layout, the same program can be used to check whether all the criteria are satisfied.

3.2.5 CEDAR

Computer synthesis at a more detailed level of design is included in the CEDAR system, which is under development in the Department of the Environment (Chalmers, 1972). So far this system has been developed to deal with structural-frame design within the SEAC building system, but is being extended to other design aspects. The frame design procedure begins with the architect indicating the structural 'bays' into which he wishes to divide the building; that is, essentially the lines along which structural columns may be placed. CEDAR will first check that this bay layout is legitimate within the SEAC rules and that no errors have been made. If there are any such errors, these can be corrected by the designer in an interactive 'dialogue' with the computer, through an on-line terminal. The design 'dialogue' will then continue with CEDAR requesting information on further design criteria, such as whether minimum cost is the ultimate objective or whether regularity of frame layout is more important.

CEDAR then completes the design of the frame, on the basis of built-in economic rules, and presents this design to the architect for approval. If the architect is not satisfied, he can modify his original bay layout and obtain another automatic frame design. Once the architect is satisfied with CEDAR's design, the program will produce a complete specifiation of the frame—it will select the appropriately sized components, print schedules, and plot working drawings. Related design work, such as the positioning of the precast concrete floor slabs and the steel roof-deck, and the design of the concrete pad foundations, will also be carried out automatically by CEDAR.

The external wall of a SEAC/CEDAR building will be designed in a similar manner, with the computer automatically selecting components and producing schedules and production drawings. Eventually most design activities will presumably be incorporated into similar CEDAR procedures. So, from site layout to detail design there appears to be little of the architectural design process that is not amenable to some degree of computer synthesis.

3.3 Computer evaluation

Of the three stages of the design process—analysis, synthesis, and evaluation—perhaps the least controversial for the application of computer aids is that of evaluation. By the time this stage is reached, most of the 'creativity' is over, and rational appraisal of the design proposal is called for. The exhaustive computational abilities of the computer can now come into their own.

Kamnitzer (1969) has clearly expressed a commonly accepted view of a legitimate need for computer evaluation in design. He points out that the complexity of modern architecture goes beyond the designer's intuitive evaluative abilities, and argues: "What is needed is a 'tool' which will permit the designer the free reign of his intuitive and creative powers (subconscious as well as conscious), yet provide him with an immediate evaluation of the costs and effects of his tentative design proposals. The essence of pertinent information from many disciplines should be at his fingertips, ready to point out the strength and weakness of each aspect of the proposed design. The designer has the choice to utilize this evaluation as he wishes: he can ignore it or use it to improve his tentative proposals until he has arrived at the highest evaluation in the greatest number of factors".

3.3.1 INTU-VAL

Such a tool is now available, Kamnitzer suggests, embodied in computer applications like his own INTU-VAL (Intuition and Evaluation), "which utilizes the computer for systematic evaluation of intuitively conceived design proposals". INTU-VAL is actually an application in transportation planning, particularly highway route location. It uses an on-line computer graphic system to display a variety of maps—showing contours, land values, geology, population, visual interest or conservation areas—on any of which the planner can sketch a route for the proposed highway. The computer will automatically locate, and display on command, this route on each of the other maps.

The planner can then obtain from INTU-VAL an evaluation of the proposed route in terms of such factors as driving time, cost, safety, visual interest, etc. These evaluations are displayed on the computer's output screen in the form of bar charts which permit instant visual comparison. Detailed analyses of each of the factors are also available. Thus, informed by this data, the planner may modify the proposal, obtain a revised set of evaluations, and so on, in an iterative process of refinement. The use of such evaluatory bar charts in architectural design has been investigated by Cakin (1976), and the approach seems likely to be adopted in various CAAD systems.

3.3.2 PACE

A basically similar intention to use the computer as an evaluation tool is embodied in the PACE program (Maver, 1971). PACE (Package for Architectural Computer Evaluation) is an 'appraisal package' which allows the designer "rapidly to appraise a large number of alternative schemes, each appraisal dealing with all quantifiable aspects of the scheme relevant to the current stage in the design activity". The quantifiable aspects are such criteria as capital, maintenance and other costs, site utilization, plan compactness, heating and lighting requirements, etc. The program is designed for interactive use, through on-line access to a time-shared computer system.

Maver prefers to regard 'appraisal' as a process wider than just 'evaluation'. In his terms, evaluation is the final stage of appraisal, which must be preceded by a measurement stage, which in turn is preceded by a representation stage. That is, a proposed design must first be represented to the computer, then its performance can be measured, and finally these measures can be evaluated against the design criteria.

In the simplest version of the PACE program, which is intended for use at the outline-proposal stage of design, the outline scheme is represented to the computer in terms of basic three-dimensional blocks located on a site. This representation is made by typing in at the computer terminal the coordinates of a pair of opposing corners for each block, together with very simple data on site locations and conditions. Further data on building type, number of occupants, construction type, areas of glazing etc are also input to the computer, which thus builds up a simple model of the proposed building, its patterns of use, and so on.

Two types of variable are used in the measurement of this model by the computer. Firstly, cost variables are either determined by 'taking off' quantities and applying standard costing procedures, or, in the case of running costs, determined by an analysis of the heating, lighting, etc loads that the building would demand. Secondly, a number of performance variables can be measured. These include spatial performance (site utilization, plan compactness, etc), environmental performance (service plant required to maintain an acceptable environment, etc), and activity performance (measures of the satisfaction of user requirements, such as the relative locations of rooms or departments in comparison with their desired proximities). The program prints out tables of the various measurements it makes of the outline scheme.

To assist the designer's evaluation of the proposed scheme PACE keeps a file of a number of previous schemes, and outputs alongside each of the measured variables a mean figure obtained from similar measurements of the previous schemes. Thus the designer can compare how well or badly his scheme relates to an average design performance for similar schemes. As with INTU-VAL the intention is that the designer will evaluate his proposal on the basis of the computer's measurements, modify the proposal, and obtain a new set of measurements, and so on until he is satisfied (or runs out of time, or patience, or becomes exhausted by the effort).

3.3.3 URBAN5
Programs such as PACE tend to assume that the designer first completes a proposed scheme, then evaluates it, then prepares a new complete scheme, evaluates that, and so on. In fact the designer may well want to evaluate

bits of an incomplete scheme, and build up to what he can be sure will be a reasonably successful scheme at first completion. This more ad hoc approach to design was recognized in the URBAN5 computer-aided design system (Negroponte and Groisser, 1970), which was regarded as an 'urban design partner' or 'a machine that discusses urban design'.

The 'discussion' that went on between the designer and URBAN5 was of the outline urban design scheme that the designer was building up on the computer's display screen. The designer could state his design criteria to the machine and 'explain' his scheme to the machine as he developed it —"this surface is opaque, this one is transparent", etc. In response the machine would keep the designer informed of any conflicts and any inconsistencies that it might discover between the criteria and the current state of the proposed scheme. It thus would keep up a constant evaluation of the scheme being developed and, if it found important criteria being violated, might even 'interrupt' the designer to point out the violation. In such a situation "URBAN5... states that a conflict has occurred, it quotes the designer's statement of criterion, and it displays the present status of the situation. From here the designer can take one of four courses: (1) he can change the form to be compatible with the criterion, (2) he can alter the criterion to be compatible with the form (now that he has learned that the issue may not be so important), (3) he can postpone the issue, or (4) he can ignore the conflict (much to the chagrin of URBAN5)."

There are some important performance variables that cannot be *directly* measured on a building plan. For instance the designer might like to know something of the probable patterns of pedestrian movement through a public building such as an airport, or the likely waiting time for a lift to answer a call in an office building, or the length of queue that might build up in a cafeteria. Many such questions of performance can be answered by first making a simulation of the behaviour of the building's occupants, services, etc in a given set of circumstances.

An elementary example of simulation was incorporated in URBAN5. Negroponte and Groisser reported that "a designer can have the machine simulate pedestrian travel between two points on the site. An 'x', the pedestrian, will prance across the screen trying to get from one point to the next, searching for a reasonable or at least feasible path. The machine will report the pedestrian's distance and time of travel or else the impossibility of the trip (through lack of enough elements with access)." Other simple simulations, such as the movement of the sun, were also incorporated into URBAN5.

3.3.4 COPLANNER
More complex simulations of behaviour and performance can be constructed using 'Monte Carlo' and other statistical probability techniques of operational research. One pioneering CAD system used such techniques

to simulate the performance of proposed hospitals. This was COPLANNER ("an acronym for computer-oriented *plan*ning, which suggests the cooperating but subordinate role played by the computer in the planning process"), developed by Souder et al. (1964).

COPLANNER's essential function is to simulate the 'commerce'—all movement of people and equipment—of any proposed hospital. To do this it first has to be supplied with the appropriate data on movement patterns. These patterns can be based on those of existing hospitals, or generated as original data for the hypothetical proposed hospital. The designer inputs these data to the computer by means of bar charts showing the frequency of movement of different classes of personnel or equipment between different locations in the hospital over a typical twenty-four-hour period. These graphs are input by drawing them on the computer's CRT display.

Once the commerce data base is established, the designer can go on to draw on the CRT his proposed outline plan of the hospital, and identify on it the various rooms, departments, locations, corridors, stairs, and lifts. COPLANNER can then be instructed to evaluate the proposed plan, using simulated commerce patterns. The computer will simulate (internally) a typical twenty-four-hours in the life of the hospital, transporting imaginary nurses, doctors, patients, trolleys, etc through the hypothetical building, and keeping records of the number of trips, the time taken, and route used for each trip. It will display the results of the simulation in the form of a variety of bar charts on command. It can also provide additional data, such as the number of times each lift or staircase was 'used'.

As with the other evaluation systems described above, the designer can use the information provided by COPLANNER to reiterate the design process until he is satisfied with the evaluation. An interesting alternative offered by COPLANNER is the possibility of considering different operational policies within a given hospital plan. The effects of varying, say, the patterns of delivering supplies or of using centralized or dispersed supply points, can be evaluated on COPLANNER just as readily as it can be used to evaluate alternative building plans. In this way CAD systems tend to be relevant to, and potentially to integrate, both the hardware of the building and the software of its operation.

3.3.5 City-Scape
A more directly 'architectural' simulation of a proposed building is the creation of straightforward visual models of the building—particularly perspective drawings. These can be made by a computer in the form of line drawings, either using a pen-and-ink plotter to produce drawings on paper, or using line displays on a screen. The latter, particularly if it is a cathode-ray-tube screen rather than a storage tube, can be coaxed to play potentially useful tricks such as rotating a perspective view so that one can see the gradual changes in the appearance of the building that occur

as one's point of view changes. This allows a qualitative evaluation of the scheme.

City-Scape (Kamnitzer, 1969) carries this sophistication further by providing the designer with a moving, coloured perspective display of the section of urban environment he is designing. This display can be made to change continuously in a simulation of walking in, through, and around that environment. The designer controls his 'walk' (that is, his current view) by means of a simple joy stick which moves the 'walker' forwards or backwards and turns him to the left or the right. A second lever offers the facility of simulated head/eye movement, and another knob controls the speed of movement. So the viewer can see the environment as it would appear during driving or walking, running, jumping, and standing still.

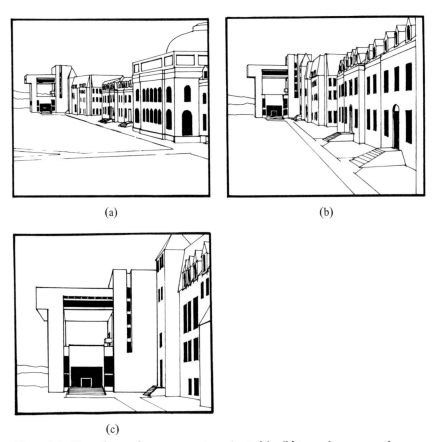

(a)   (b)

(c)

Figure 3.4. Three frames from a computer-animated 'walk' towards a proposed new building situated amongst existing buildings. The actual computer pictures show coloured surfaces rather than these line diagrams. (Source: Greenberg, 1974).

Greenberg (1974) reported some advances in this kind of visual display technique, and commented: "A system that produces computer-generated images in colour offers three major advantages over the standard architectural drawings and models. They are flexibility in changing the design, the ability to simulate motion, and the opportunity to change and experiment with colour... For architects the ability to simulate motion is highly useful. One of the principal concerns of architectural design is space... To obtain a deeper understanding of architectural space it is necessary to move through the space, experiencing new views and discovering the sequence of complex spatial relations". Highly simplified versions of the City-Scape or Greenberg's type of display are shown in figure 3.4.

Both quantitative and qualitative evaluations of proposed designs are therefore possible with the computer. Perhaps the most significant aspect of computer evaluation is that it has the potential to eliminate much of the guesswork in design and the uncertainty of not knowing what a building will really be like until it has been built. Whether architects will in fact be able to respond to the elimination of guesswork and cope with the loss of uncertainty is another matter.

3.4 An integrated example

The following 'worked example' illustrates a computer-aided architectural design system in which analysis, synthesis, and evaluation are integrated in one compatible 'suite' of programs. The example chosen is that of the SPACES suite developed at the Architecture and Building Aids Computer Unit, Strathclyde (ABACUS). SPACES is intended specifically as an aid in the design of schools at the preliminary design stage. Its component programs, SPACES 1, SPACES 2, and SPACES 3, provide aids to analysis, synthesis, and evaluation, respectively.

3.4.1 SPACES 1

The first program is concerned with the analysis of spatial requirements for the proposed school. Part of the justification for this particular program is that there is often a considerable mismatch between the accommodation provided in a school and the actual spatial needs of the teachers and pupils. SPACES 1 provides a means of establishing a more exact fit between needs and provision, in terms both of overall space and of the variety of rooms provided. This does require, however, a detailed preanalysis of the curriculum to be implemented in the school, including the subjects to be studied, the group compositions within each subject, their spatial requirements, the percentage time allocated to each subject-group, etc.

The designer interacts with the computer program by means of a CRT screen and an associated keyboard. The computer initiates the design 'dialogue' with a short sequence of questions (figure 3.5). 'Percent maximum space utilisation' establishes just how tight a fit between spatial needs and spatial provision the designer wants to achieve. The lower this figure, the looser is the fit and the greater is the overall accommodation that needs to be provided. A further two questions establish which year-groups the designer is designing for, and whether any shared use of common spaces is to be included.

The output which immediately follows (figure 3.6) is a detailed schedule of accommodation, including the percentage utilization of each space that will occur. Obviously, the designer can reiterate this procedure, changing the year-groups to be considered (for example, dividing into upper and lower schools), the use of shared spaces, and the maximum space utilization. In each case, the accommodation schedule is likely to vary, and thus the spatial implications of different policies can be explored. Each run of this program costs approximately £5 (1974 prices for this and subsequent estimates in this example) and takes a few minutes.

```
HEADINGS ON ALL PAGES? 0/1
>1

PERCENT MAXIMUM SPACE UTILISATION
>80
 TYPE IN NO OF YEARS IN GROUP AND ACTUAL YEARS
>5,1,2,3,4,5
 NO OF GROUPS OF COMBINED SPACES
>0
```

Figure 3.5.

>

SUBJECT	SPACE TYPE	NO OF SPACES	AREA OF EACH SPACE	TOTAL AREA	AVE SEAT UTIL	SPACE UTIL
MATHS	GENERA	2	49		87.8	80.0
		1	31	129	75.2	42.0
MATHS	STUDY	2	51		97.3	80.0
		2	48		96.8	80.0
		2	39	276	97.9	72.0
MATHS	M.LAB.	1	83		85.7	80.0
		1	67	150	80.6	72.0
BUS.ST	GENERA	1	31	31	79.1	68.0
BUS.ST	TYPING	1	45	45	87.2	59.0
BUS.ST	PROJEC	1	52	52	87.3	70.0
BUS.ST	OFFICE	1	41	41	88.5	64.0
SCIENC	LECT.	2	24	48	98.6	78.0
SCIENC	GENLAB	5	56	280	99.3	79.0
SCIENC	CHELAB	1	56		96.7	80.0
		1	53	109	86.9	44.0
SCIENC	PHYLAB	1	56		96.0	80.0
		1	53	109	55.8	13.0
SCIENC	BIOLAB	1	56		97.8	80.0
		1	53	109	85.2	39.0

Figure 3.6.

A summary table of total areas (figure 3.7) is also provided. Any display on the screen can be reproduced as 'hard copy'—that is, printed on paper—for reference.

SUBJECT	AREA(SQ.M)	%
MATHS	555	8.5
BUS.ST	169	2.6
SCIENC	743	11.4
TECH.	668	10.3
ART	476	7.3
H.ECON	372	5.7
ENGLIS	738	11.4
LANG.	394	6.1
CLASIC	193	3.0
SOCIAL	501	7.7
MUSIC	278	4.3
P.E.	1226	18.9
RE/REM	181	2.8
S1/S2	0	.0
TOTAL	6494	100.0

>

Figure 3.7.

3.4.2 SPACES 2
Once the required spatial provision has been decided, the designer can move on to the synthesis of a spatial arrangement. Additional data required for this in the SPACES 2 program are the appropriate planning constraints (specific orientation required for any particular spaces, adjacencies, or explicit nonadjacencies required, etc) and the association

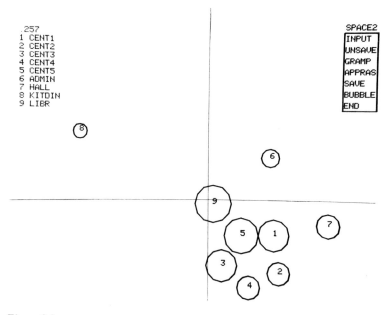

Figure 3.8.

relationships between the spaces (that is, an interaction matrix indicating for each pair of spaces the strength of the desirability for that pair to be close together in the final arrangement).

SPACES 2 begins the spatial arrangement process in a manner familiar to all architects—the use of simple 'bubble' diagrams in which each 'bubble' represents a space to be provided and is drawn approximately in proportion to the required size of that space. The SPACES-2 bubble diagram (figure 3.8) is generated by the program with the use of the MDS technique, which positions each bubble so that the distance between each pair is inversely proportional to its value in the interaction matrix. From this rough, but rational, start provided by the computer, the designer can shuffle the bubbles around to his liking. In the top left-hand corner of the screen is a 'score' which changes after each move to indicate how close to the 'ideal' (a zero score) the bubble diagram remains. The point of the bubble diagram is that it enables the designer to formulate a strategy, or concept, for the spatial arrangement before moving to a more realistic sketch.

The bubble diagram is converted to a rectangular format (figure 3.9) when the designer is ready to proceed further. On the right of the screen appears a 'menu' of commands from which the designer may select in order to manipulate the spatial arrangement. The MOVE command, for example, enables any space to be moved to a new location. The new location is indicated by the designer positioning a pair of 'crosswires'

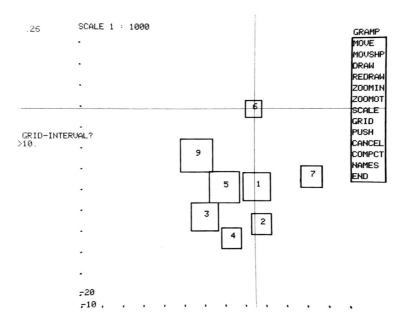

Figure 3.9.

(horizontal and vertical lines on the screen, moved by a pair of thumbwheels on the keyboard) at the bottom-left corner of the desired location. The SCALE command will cause the layout to be redrawn at a stated new scale (figure 3.10).

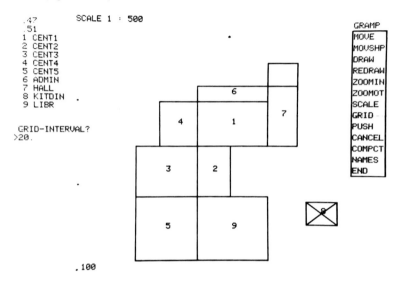

Figure 3.10.

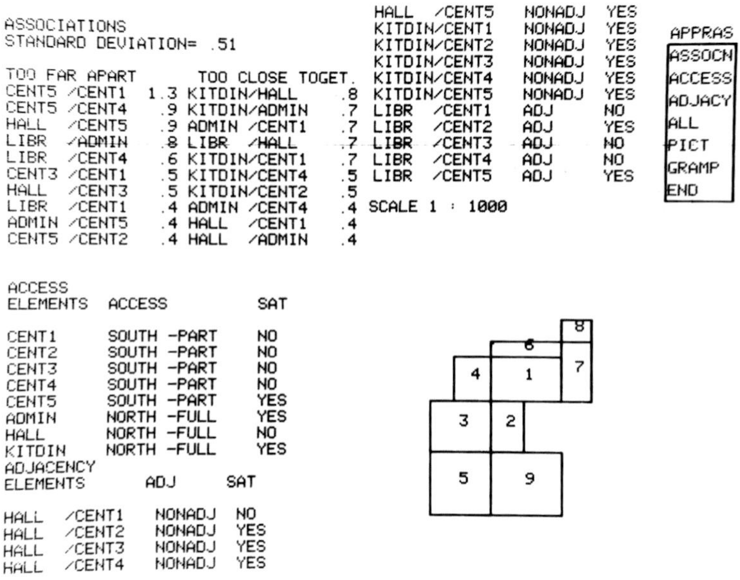

Figure 3.11.

The designer is kept informed of the efficiency of his spatial arrangement by the 'score' in the top left-hand corner of the screen. At any time he may also call for a brief evaluation of the layout as it stands (figure 3.11). Three tables inform him of the current association, access, and adjacency aspects of the layout. The first table lists the worst ten pairs of spaces, from those that are still relatively far apart from each other (based on the interaction matrix data), and also the worst ten pairs that might be said to be, conversely, closer together than they need be. In the second table is an indication of whether the access requirements (full or partial access in specified directions, for designated spaces) are satisfied. The third table similarly records whether the various adjacency/nonadjacency requirements are satisfied.

Continuing in this way, the designer can switch between bubble diagram, sketch, and constraints tables in any sequence—perhaps developing a number of tentative proposals, each of which can be stored in computer files. Since most of the time during the operation of SPACES 2 is taken up with the designer's manipulation of the layout on the screen, computer costs are quite low—around £15 for a couple of hours' operation.

3.4.3 SPACES 3
The simple evaluation available with SPACES 2 is limited to the planning aspects of the constraints tables. In SPACES 3 a more comprehensive evaluation of the proposed scheme is available. This evaluation depends on standard (or else specially input) data files held in the computer in respect of, for example, the environmental performance of certain building constructional types. A small range only of industrialised systems is currently available on file in SPACES 3 for the designer to select from (figure 3.12). Basic site data, the date of expected tender for the scheme, etc, are elicited from the designer by the computer, in order that it can

```
------------------------------------------------------------------------
SPACES 3
------------------------------------------------------------------------

DO YOU WISH TO CHANGE FILES
0=NO
1=YES SCOLA
2=YES CLASP
3=YES MACE
>0
                                                 ------------------------
INPUT: GENERAL
------------------------------------------------------------------------

SITE REFERENCE,AVERAGE HEIGHT OF SITE,MONTHS TO TENDER
>2,50,12

ORIENTATION: ANGLE BETWEEN Y AXIS AND TRUE NORTH
>22.

NUMBER OF PUPILS
>750
       -----------------------------------------------------------------
>
```

Figure 3.12.

adjust its data files to allow for site exposure, the effects of inflation on costs, etc.

A very brief summary table of the scheme under consideration is first output by SPACES 3 (figure 3.13). It then goes on, if the designer so desires, to evaluate the activity performance—that is, how well the spatial arrangement has been planned with respect to the interaction-matrix data. (Note that in figure 3.13 the designer indicates that the matrix is already on file by typing the file reference number in response to the request to "type association of components".) The output table (figure 3.14) of the ten pairs of spaces that are either 'too far apart' or 'too close together' is similar to that available in SPACES 2. A more detailed evaluation is also available here, however, in the form of a matrix giving the association 'score' for every pair of spaces (figure 3.15).

```
----------------------------------------------------------------------------
OUTPUT : GENERAL
----------------------------------------------------------------------------

                                    SQ.M
TOTAL FLOOR AREA                  1263.60
TOTAL EXTERNAL WALL                721.44
TOTAL ROOF AREA                   1263.60
WALL TO FLOOR RATIO                             .57
VOLUME COMPACTNESS                              .48

----------------------------------------------------------------------------

DO YOU WISH TO CHANGE GEOMETRY
>0

DO YOU WISH TO ANALYSE ACTIVITY
>1

----------------------------------------------------------------------------
INPUT ACTIVITY
----------------------------------------------------------------------------

TYPE ASSOCIATION OF COMPONENTS
>@ADD LINK*SP3ASS.
```

Figure 3.13.

```
----------------------------------------------------------------------------
OUTPUT : ACTIVITY PERFORMANCE
----------------------------------------------------------------------------

STANDARD DEVIATION =     .562

   TOO FAR APART                        TOO CLOSE TOGETHER
   COMPONENTS    DEVIATION              COMPONENTS    DEVIATION
CENTR5/CENTR1      1.51              LIBRA./HALL        .88
CENTR4/CENTR1       .99              KITDIN/HALL        .81
LIBRA./CENTR3       .90              LIBRA./KITDIN      .78
CENTR5/CENTR2       .86              KITDIN/ADMIN       .68
HALL /CENTR3        .82              ADMIN /CENTR5      .66
CENTR3/CENTR1       .58              KITDIN/CENTR1      .54
CENTR5/CENTR3       .45              KITDIN/CENTR5      .51
LIBRA./CENTR4       .43              HALL /ADMIN        .50
HALL /CENTR4        .43              KITDIN/CENTR2      .35
LIBRA./CENTR5       .36              ADMIN /CENTR2      .35

----------------------------------------------------------------------------

DO YOU WISH TO SEE COMPLETE MATRIX
>1
```

Figure 3.14.

In this matrix a high positive number indicates that the corresponding pair is too far apart; a high negative number indicates that they are unnecessarily close.

Next, the designer specifies (figure 3.16) the building system to be used, indicating the type of cladding panels, etc which will predominate as the 'standard construction', together with exceptions to this standard. Using the data now established, the computer can provide an evaluation of the environmental performance of the proposed scheme. This evaluation includes an identification of the worst ten wall surfaces in respect both of heat loss and of heat gain (figure 3.17), and estimates of permanent artificial lighting, boiler, and water-storage requirements (figure 3.18).

```
        CENTR1   CENTR2   CENTR3   CENTR4   CENTR5   ADMIN    HALL     KITDIN
CENTR2   -.25
CENTR3    .58    -.17
CENTR4    .99     .34     -.28
CENTR5   1.51     .86      .45     -.17
ADMIN    -.08    -.35      .06     -.25     -.66
HALL      .06     .30      .82      .43     -.08     -.50
KITDIN   -.54    -.35     -.15     -.30     -.51     -.68     -.81
LIBRA.   -.28     .28      .90      .43      .36     -.29     -.88     -.78
```

```
DO YOU WISH TO CHANGE GEOMETRY
>0
```

Figure 3.15.

```
INPUT: CONSTRUCTION
```

```
BUILDING SYSTEM, FUEL TYPE
>1,4
```

```
STANDARD CONSTRUCTION
>19,10,1,6,2,2
```

```
EXCEPTIONS TO STANDARD CONSTRUCTION
END WITH 0,0,0,0,0,0
>@ADD LINK*SP3EX.
```

Figure 3.16.

```
DO YOU WISH TO ANALYSE ENVIRONMENTAL PERFORMANCES
>1
```

```
OUTPUT: ENVIRONMENTAL PERFORMANCE
```

```
HEAT LOSS (JANUARY)                  HEAT GAIN (JULY)
COMPONENT    SURFACE    W/SQ.M       COMPONENT    SURFACE    W/SQ.M
CENTR2 1     NORTH       75.7        CENTR3 1     EAST        332.7
CENTR3 1     EAST        59.0        LIBRA. 1     WEST        331.0
LIBRA. 1     EAST        56.6        CENTR1 1     SOUTH       315.4
LIBRA. 1     WEST        52.7        LIBRA. 1     EAST        293.2
CENTR1 1     WEST        51.0        CENTR1 1     WEST        291.6
CENTR3 1     WEST        51.0        CENTR3 1     WEST        291.6
ADMIN  2     NORTH       34.6        CENTR3 1     SOUTH       213.9
HALL   1     NORTH       34.6        CENTR2 1     SOUTH       165.8
KITDIN 1     NORTH       34.6        LIBRA. 1     SOUTH       101.6
CENTR3 1     NORTH       34.6        HALL   1     EAST         64.4

             AVERAGE     25.1                     AVERAGE     119.3
             TOTAL      652.6                     TOTAL      3103.1
```

```
>
```

Figure 3.17.

c

```
-----------------------------------------------------------------------
PERMANENT ARTIFICIAL LIGHTING

SQ.M=  632.2
%  =   50.0

-----------------------------------------------------------------------
BOILER CONFIGURATION

TOTAL CAPACITY(KW)   NUMBER   SIZE(M)        ROOM SIZE(M)
2300                 3        3.7 X 1.8      13.7 X 9.1 X 4.6

-----------------------------------------------------------------------
COLD WATER STORAGE

LITRES= 16139.2
CU.M =    16.1
-----------------------------------------------------------------------
>
```

Figure 3.18.

```
-----------------------------------------------------------------------
OUTPUT: COSTS
-----------------------------------------------------------------------

                            $        %       $/SQ.M    $/PUPIL
HEATING COST               573.     27.9       .45
LIGHTING COST              710.     34.5       .56
MAINTENANCE COST           455.     22.1       .36
HOT WATER COST             319.     15.5       .25
RUNNING COST              2057.    100.0      1.63

CAPITAL COST            104585.                82.77    139.45
D.E.S. COST LIMIT       165000.               130.58    220.00
ACTUAL COST             110860.                87.73    147.81
ANNUAL EQUIVALENT        12187.                 9.64     16.25

-----------------------------------------------------------------------

DO YOU WISH TO SEE COST BREAKDOWN
>1
```

Figure 3.19.

```
-----------------------------------------------------------------------
ELEMENTAL COSTS

                                    $        %      $/SQ.M
A    GENERAL                      9035.     8.6      7.15
BC   FOUNDATIONS                 11992.    11.5      9.49
D    FRAME                        6571.     6.3      5.20
E    ROOFS AND ROOF LIGHTS       19723.    18.9     15.61
F    EXTERNAL WALL AND DOORS     14870.    14.2     11.77
G    INTERNAL WALLS               9338.     8.9      7.39
H    UPPER FLOORS                    0.      .0       .00
I    STAIRCASES                      0.      .0       .00
J    FIXTURES                     4612.     4.4      3.65
K    WATER,SANITARY INSTALLATI.   7026.     6.7      5.56
M    HEATING INSTALLATIONS        9035.     8.6      7.15
N    MECHANICAL                    480.      .5       .38
O    ELECTRICAL                   5244.     5.0      4.15
R    GAS                           468.      .4       .37
S    EXTERNAL SERVICES            2856.     2.7      2.26
T    DRAINAGE                     3336.     3.2      2.64
-----------------------------------------------------------------------
>
```

Figure 3.20.

Estimated capital and running costs are also available (figure 3.19—note that the $ sign should be read as a £ sign; most computers seem to be congenitally incapable of typing any currency symbol other than the $).

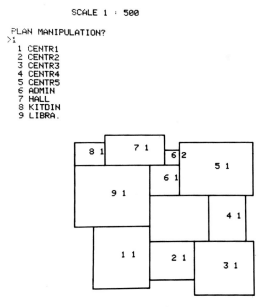

Figure 3.21.

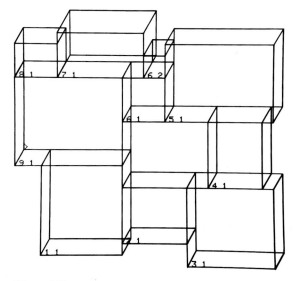

Figure 3.22.

A further breakdown of the estimated capital costs into sixteen constructional elements can be provided (figure 3.20).

At any time during the use of SPACES 3 the geometry of the scheme can be changed (figure 3.21). On request, the computer can also provide axonometric (figure 3.22) or perspective drawings of the scheme. One complete run of SPACES 3 costs approximately £6.

Thus, for relatively low overall cost, the SPACES suite of programs provides an integrated analysis, synthesis, and evaluation of a proposed scheme at a preliminary design stage. Other program suites with basic similarities with SPACES, but for use at sketch design and detail design stages, are being developed by ABACUS. A more general account of SPACES is given by Th'ng and Davies (1975).

3.5 The machine as architect
The undoubted relevance and usefulness of computer aids to architectural design has encouraged some research workers to pursue the application of CAD to its apparently logical conclusion—giving the machine facilities, skills, and independence until it can be regarded as a virtual architect in its own right.

Obviously, many of the facilities and skills already exist, if only in an embryonic form in some instances, but the real difficulty lies in giving the machine its independence. This is a problem that is bound up with the whole field of artificial intelligence, which promised major advances in the early and mid-1960s, but which, more than a decade later, is still struggling with brutish machines that remain stubbornly moronic.

3.5.1 The machine as hero
Despite the awesome difficulties, since the later 1960s Negroponte and his colleagues at the MIT Department of Architecture have "adopted the position that computer-aided architecture had to be treated as an issue of machine intelligence". Their experiments, trials, successes, and failures have been subsumed into a continuous project to create 'the Architecture Machine' (Negroponte, 1970; 1975). There is naturally great uncertainty as to when, or whether, the Architecture Machine will emerge as a complete, independent entity—Negroponte seems to have taken it on as a life's work. However, a variety of potential facilities and skills have been developed for it.

The Architecture Machine project rose from the ashes of URBAN5 (Negroponte and Groisser, 1970), the 'urban design partner'. This partner was eventually unplugged because of its basic inadequacies. It was seen to contain undesirable biases towards certain interpretations of the nature of architecture and design; it was a collection of specific little machines and not a general-purpose machine; it did not admit a necessary ambiguity and contextual overlap in the design process; it could not interact with the world except through highly constrained communication with the designer.

After cataloguing these failures of URBAN5, Negroponte (1970) does add, however: "Any postmortem statement should do some eulogizing. Even though URBAN5 was a bit talkative and was a sloppy problem solver, it *was* a friendly system".

From this apparent false start with URBAN5, the Architecture Machine Group went on to conduct a series of fascinating experiments aimed at demonstrating or finding the inklings of machine intelligence in the context of architectural design. Their ideal was a concept of an architecture machine which "must understand our metaphors, must solicit information on its own, must acquire experiences, must talk to a wide variety of people, must improve over time, and must be intelligent" (Negroponte, 1970). They wanted to build machines "that can learn, can grope, and can fumble".

Towards this end, the group built a number of small machines and devices. SEE is an exercise in machine vision, in which a computer is programmed to look at three-dimensional arrangements of blocks by means of a video lens, and then to try to draw on a CRT, what it reckons it has seen. GROPE is a mobile light sensor (based on a toy tank) which crawls over a surface such as a map, looking for 'interesting' features. GREET is a doorway which tries to recognize whoever passes through it. HUNCH is an experiment in programming the computer to recognize sketches, so that it can realize, as a designer is in the act of sketching, whether he is being vague or precise about the intentions of each part of the sketch. SEEK is a model environment constructed of small cubes that can be arranged and rearranged by an arm on an overhead gantry; the environment has been inhabited by gerbils, and SEEK valiantly attempted to maintain and modify the arrangement of cubes as they were shifted by the gerbils' activities. The gerbils' response to this 'deus ex machina' continually descending into their lives from above was, as one might expect, not recorded.

These ingenious experiments may someday lead to a robot architect; but then, so might the more conventional CAD experiments. Negroponte's concern is that the results of the conventional approaches would be 'unethical robots', machines that "would do only the dull, ignoble tasks,... employing only the procedures and the information designers explicitly give them... these machines would have the built-in prejudices and 'default options' of their creators" (Negroponte, 1970). He suggests that much CAD work only produces faster ways of doing what designers already do. "And since what designers already do does not seem to work, we will get inbred methods of work that will make bad architecture, unresponsive architecture, even more prolific."

3.5.2 The machine as villain
Negroponte is not alone in fearing that computer-aided design will mean the proliferation of bad architecture. Some would see a danger in the

often inflated claims made for minor developments in CAD, claims which might lead to their unwitting adoption by design practioners. [The claims are frequently enhanced by the use of esoteric name shrouds; as Eberhard (1970) commented, every little research development "has to have its own acronym—even if it's words like CHEAP, QUICK, or even JUNK".] Some would suspect that the computer is being applied in areas where its abilities are simply irrelevant, and that the efficiency of the *process* will be allowed to overshadow the quality of the *product*.

Alexander (1965), despite his own earlier use of the computer as a design aid, has vehemently criticized certain applications of CAD which are based on what he regards as pointless quantification for its own sake. He objected that it was "like measuring the size of a cooking apple with a micrometer". "A digital computer", he said, "is, essentially, the same as a huge army of clerks, equipped with rule books, pencil and paper, all stupid and entirely without initiative, but able to follow exactly millions of precisely defined operations.... In asking how the computer might be applied to architectural design, we must, therefore, ask ourselves what problems we know of in design that could be solved by such an army of clerks.... At the moment, there are very few such problems."

However, Alexander went on to distinguish his own objections to the use of computer aids from those of some other designers who merely fear a threat to their personal intuitive and creative design autonomy. "Those who fear the computer itself are invariably those who regard design as an opportunity for personal expression." He was still prepared to use a computer where it might help the designer to deal with the relationship between the complexities of form and the complexities of function.

No doubt many designers continue to regard computers as brainless 'armies of clerks', despite the brave attempts by Negroponte and others to show that these machines can be quite intelligent and friendly. Everyone's personal, everyday experiences with computers (for example with computer-produced bills or bank accounts) probably tend to confirm the pejorative view of computers. Moonman (1971), for instance, has outlined a number of expensive computer system failures and notes that seventy per cent of computer systems in industry and commerce "fail to do properly the job intended." Even Negroponte (1975) acknowledges that problems with computer typesetting greatly delayed publication of his book, *Soft Architecture Machines.*

Alexander (1971) later went further in his criticism of CAD—particularly on-line applications such as the use of computer graphics. He said he would argue "very strongly against computer graphics simply because of the frame of mind that you need to be in to create a good building. Are you thinking about smell and touch, and what happens when people are walking about in a place?... All that is completely disturbed by the pretentiousness, insistence and complicatedness of computer graphics and all the allied techniques."

However, in architectural design, computer applications frequently have been orientated toward 'overlooked' design tasks, such as lighting, heating, and acoustic calculations, attention to which ought to improve the performance of buildings. This orientation suggests that computer-aided designing may produce better results than manual designing, despite fears that computer-designed buildings will actually make rather dismal architecture. But on investigating the grounds for such fears, Archer (1972) was "reluctantly compelled to conclude that under present conditions CAAD does *not* permit the architect to improve his performance in the handling of the qualitative... When the first generation of CAAD buildings is exposed before the critical gaze of the non-committed public, the occasion could be a signal for another outburst, more or less justified, of accusations of a further de-humanising of the built environment". Perhaps significantly, there is a growing tendency amongst the research workers to talk of computer-aided *building* design, rather than architectural design (for example Eastman, 1975).

Unimpressed even by the Architecture Machine, Kahn (1973) has expressed rather more forcefully his feelings about the likely environment to be created by the machine as architect: "It's going to look like shit—guaranteed—and it will only produce environments that machines or machine-like people will want to inhabit".

Part 2

Humans versus machines

"Yes", said Rowe. "That's really the basic, er, the basic..."

"...principle on which our work is founded....

"...Filling up a football coupon is another job which a computer could easily be programmed to do. You could set it to fill the coupon at random, or to make a selection based on any system you liked, or to select its own system, or to choose between a random choice and a system of its own choosing. Once again we have a range of variables which can be identified in advance and manipulated according to predetermined rules. It's programmable. Having a man to perform it is a waste of time."

"Y-e-e-es." said Rowe. "Y-e-e-es."

"And when you come to think about it, you could programme a computer to appreciate the cricket results for you—or even to appreciate the actual automated game as the playing computer played it. It would be instructed to register applause at amazing freaks—at, say, the announcement of a slip catch off a fast bowler in poor light. It would register annoyance when the side it was instructed to identify with suffered a reverse— annoyance mixed with reluctant admiration if it was the result of the other side's skill. It would be programmed to register boredom when nothing unusual happened for some time—without any boredom being inflicted on any actual human being."

Human–computer interaction

4.1 The symbiotic partnership

Computer applications have mushroomed so dramatically (between 1960 and 1970 the numbers of computers in use multiplied nearly thirty times) and are now so pervasive that it is easy to forget that it was not until the 1960s that anyone other than a few specialist engineers or programmers ever 'communicated' with computers. The earliest (in the late 1940s) forms of this man–machine communication were numerical machine codes. In the 1950s these codes were gradually superseded by primitive computer programming 'languages', but it was not until the 1960s that high-level languages enabled nonspecialist users to have access to computers. Even the widespread computer applications of the 1970s do not permit much more man–machine 'communication' than may be possible through a standardized format of predetermined question–answer interrogation.

It is therefore perhaps a considerable leap of imagination that Negroponte (1970) requests:

"Imagine a machine that can follow your design methodology and at the same time discern and assimilate your conversational idiosyncracies. This same machine, after observing your behaviour, could build a predictive model of your conversational performance. Such a machine could then reinforce the dialogue by using the predictive model to respond to you in a manner that is in rhythm with your personal behaviour and conversational idiosyncracies... The dialogue would be so intimate— even exclusive—that only mutual persuasion and compromise would bring about ideas, ideas unrealizable by either conversant alone. No doubt, in such a symbiosis it would not be solely the human designer who would decide when the machine is relevant."

The concept of such a symbiosis is not a new one; Negroponte is only applying it in a new, architectural-design, context. The concept of 'man–computer symbiosis' was first presented by Licklider (1960), who expressed the hope that, "in not too many years, human brains and computing machines will be coupled together very tightly, and that the resulting partnership will think as no human brain has ever thought and process data in a way not approached by the information-handling machines we know today".

The basis of this hope was that heuristic aspects of problem solving need not be separated from algorithmic aspects—that is, that human abilities and machine abilities could mesh with and complement each other. The difference between heuristic and algorithmic problem solving is that an algorithm is a step-by-step mechanical procedure guaranteed to identify the single correct or optimum solution to a problem, whereas an heuristic involves trial-and-error procedures or an element of chance as the only way

of finding an 'acceptable' solution (within certain limits) to a complex or
ill-defined problem.

Later, Licklider (1965) suggested that the separation of these two
problem-solving modes "would be a source of amazement... to a student
of problem solving who had not been conditioned by the development of
computing during the last twenty years". At that time there was much
enthusiasm for concepts of "computer augmentation of human reasoning"
(Sass and Wilkinson, 1965) and the machine as "an amplifier of the mental
abilities of the brain" (Yershov, 1965).

However, Newell (1965) suggested that it is not so much that problem
solving is hampered by being split into heuristic and algorithmic modes,
but that these modes represent the state of knowledge about how to solve
a particular type of problem. That is, if it is known how to solve a problem,
then it is solved algorithmically, but if there is no known algorithm, then
it has to be solved heuristically. Newell's argument thus casts some doubt
on the relevance of striving for a symbiotic human–machine partnership.

Licklider (1965) identified the practical difficulties of "forging a
successful intellectual partnership of man and computer" as being the
"speed–cost mismatch" and the "language mismatch". The speed–cost
mismatch meant that "only under extraordinary circumstances does it
make sense to let a slow-thinking, low-paid man monopolize a fast,
expensive computer". The language mismatch meant that people who
were not skilled in an artificial computer programming language could not
hope to 'converse' with the machine, anyway.

4.1.1 Interactive systems

These two difficulties have since been overcome to a considerable extent
by the development of, firstly, time-sharing computer systems and,
secondly, high-level or problem-orientated languages. In a time-shared
computer system many users have access, through their individual consoles,
to one 'fast, expensive' computer in an apparently simultaneous manner.
The computer in fact divides its attention among all the connected users.

The earliest time-sharing systems, such as the MAC system (Fano, 1965)
or the JOSS system (Shaw, 1964), were established around 1963 in
universities and research establishments, but soon became commercially
available also. (TELCOMP was available from Time-Sharing Ltd. in Britain
in 1967.) In combination with the development of related languages (such
as BASIC), and other high-level languages, time-sharing systems have
promoted an 'interactive' computer use. Most computer-aided architectural
design systems now rely on this interactive mode to allow at least a
primitive form of 'dialogue' between man and machine.

There is still no evidence, though, of a human–machine 'symbiosis'
emerging, such as Licklider and Negroponte expressed their hopes for.
Davis (1966) noted that "very little has been written on the effectiveness
of time-shared systems as a means to improving man–computer interaction",

and questioned the view that "man–machine interaction, per se, will result in either augmentation of human intellect or reduction of the artificial separation of algorithmic and heuristic aspects of problem solving". This view remains under question and unverified. Nickerson (1969), after "a careful search", had to conclude that "in short, there is remarkably little evidence of research that has been undertaken for the express purpose either of increasing our understanding of man–computer interaction or of providing information that will be useful in the development of systems that are optimally suited to users' needs and preferences".

Similarly, Vaughan and Schumacher-Mavor (1972) ask, "where are the user-oriented guidelines that will help solve design problems for this qualitatively different (conversationally interactive) man–machine circumstance? Although ten years have elapsed since Licklider (1960) and Yntema and Torgerson (1961) alerted us to the coming generation of systems based on concepts of 'man–computer symbiosis' and 'man–computer co-operation', remarkably little attention has been given to this critical issue."

Sackman (1970) too notes that, "although the enhancement of the human intellect with computers has been the subject of much speculation, remarkably little solid scientific work has been done in man–computer problem-solving. The humanistic lag in the application of computers to social affairs goes hand in hand with the experimental lag in man–computer communication." Thus it seems that there is little evidence on whether or not human–computer interaction is even effective, let alone 'symbiotic'.

4.2 Evaluation of computer systems
The reviewers echo each other that "remarkably little" research has been conducted to evaluate computer systems. The literature on basic ergonomic research (such matters as the design of hardware for input and output devices) has been reviewed by Shackel and Shipley (1970), but the absence of literature on the effectiveness of computer systems as problem-solving aids remains. Shaw (1965) collected some basic data on user behaviour with the JOSS time-sharing system. These data showed only such facts as that the average time a user spent in any one session was fifty-eight minutes. Similar, but more detailed, data were collected for the MAC system by Scherr (1966).

4.2.1 Response time
A specific problem area identified by Scherr was the effect of system response time on user behaviour. As more users attempt simultaneously to use a time-sharing system, the response time (the delay between the end of a user's input message and the beginning of the computer's corresponding output) lengthens. Scherr reckoned that the maximum acceptable number of users on the MAC system at any time was thirty, for a corresponding average response time of ten seconds.

Carbonell et al (1968) took up the issue of system response time and suggested that there was a need for research on the topic. System designers tend to assume that response time should always be as fast as may be possible in the circumstances and therefore will vary with factors such as load on the system and the type of command being executed. However, as Nickerson (1969) pointed out, the 'frustration' felt by a user in waiting for system response may be caused more by the *variability* of response time than by its mean duration.

In a specific study of the effect of response time on the problem-solving behaviour of users of an on-line computer system, Yntema et al (1969) found that, even with regular response times, user performance *was* adversely affected as the time lengthened. In particular they found that the net completion time for a problem (the total time taken to solve the problem, less the total response delay time) increased significantly with long response time (beyond thirty seconds). They concluded that "long delays apparently distract the subject or make him lose the thread of his thought". This finding is contrary to the belief of "the system designers who have suggested, rather wistfully, that delays may not be too harmful because the user will be thinking during the delays".

In an assessment of more subjective user reaction to response time, Miller (1968) found that a response time of fifteen seconds could be nearly intolerable for the user. Sackman's (1970) conclusion on 'system effectiveness', from a survey of available data on user characteristics in time-sharing systems, was that: "Users with tasks requiring relatively small computation become increasingly uncomfortable as computer response time to their requests extends beyond ten seconds and as irregularity and uncertainty of computer response time increases; users with problems requiring much computation tolerate longer intervals, up to as much as ten minutes for the largest jobs".

4.2.2 On-line vs off-line
The studies reported above do not, however, attempt to assess the relative effectiveness of different computer systems. The major work which has been done in this area involved comparisons of on-line systems with off-line systems. On-line systems are the interactive (usually time-shared) systems discussed above; off-line systems are the conventional batch-processing computer systems in which the user hands to a computer operator his complete tape or set of cards and receives the computer output usually some hours (perhaps a day) later. Controversy arises over these different systems because on-line systems are usually more expensive (but claimed to be more useful) than off-line systems.

The first comparative study was that conducted by Grant and Sackman (1967) on the System Development Corporation's Time-sharing System (TSS), in which TSS was used both for the on-line and off-line (in simulated batch-processing, with a two-hour turnaround time) modes.

In this experiment, two groups of six programmers solved two programming problems each, using the on-line mode for one problem, and the off-line mode for the other. In terms of man-hours it was concluded from this experiment that the on-line mode was significantly and substantially more efficient than the off-line mode. However, there were considerable differences between subjects. In a similar study, which also used TSS, Erikson (1966) also found significant differences between performances of the subject groups, with interactive computer use resulting in fewer man-hours and less computing time.

A comparison of an actual (as opposed to simulated) off-line batch-processing system with an on-line interactive system was conducted by Schatzoff et al (1967). With a small sample of four subjects tackling four programming problems, they found that subjects using the batch-processing system needed significantly fewer man-hours to solve the problems (less than half the man-hours used on the time-sharing system), but used slightly more computer time. Again this study found that individual performance differences tended to be larger than differences between systems.

This latter study did not report on user preferences, but both previous studies reported preference for the time-sharing mode. Herskowitz and Sankaran (1969) investigated the preferences of graduate students using computer programs for designing electronic circuits under on-line and batch-processing modes. They found that "a major difference in understanding and enthusiasm was demonstrated by students using the interactive programs with on-line, time-sharing terminals, compared with those students who used these programs on the batch-processing machines".

Two studies have used 'instant' batch (in which turnaround time is only a few minutes at most) as one of the comparison modes. Smith (1967) used it in comparison with normal batch-processing; that is, 'instant' batch was used as a simulation of an on-line system. Adams and Cohen (1969), however, used 'instant' batch as the batch-processing mode for comparison with an on-line system. Again, both studies used programming exercises as the problem type. Smith found that with 'instant' batch, subjects used approximately 20% fewer man-hours, but approximately 50% more computer time, and he reported a user preference for the 'instant' batch mode. Adams and Cohen also found a user preference for 'instant' batch, although they were comparing it with time-sharing. They found that time-sharing used slightly more man-hours, and that it seemed to have no particular advantage over the 'instant' batch mode. Individual subject differences again overshadowed system differences.

These various comparative studies tend to conflict in their findings more often than they agree. In general, problem solving in a man–machine interactive mode seems to use fewer man-hours but more computer time than an off-line mode, with the result that overall costs are approximately the same for the two modes. However, there is a strong user dislike of conventional batch-processing.

None of these studies compare the *qualities* of solutions produced in the different modes of computer use. This seems a surprising lack when one considers the hopes and claims discussed above for man–computer 'symbiosis'.

4.2.3 Evaluation of solutions

Only one study in fact seems to have set out to compare the solutions produced by subjects solving problems with the aid of on-line computer systems with those produced by subjects using off-line systems. Gold (1967) compared two matched groups of thirty students, one group using the MAC time-sharing system, and the other group using a batch-processing system with a minimum turnaround time of six hours. Each subject worked separately on the set problem, which was based on a computerized simulation model of the construction industry and its market; the subject's task was to maximize his profit in this market (as an independent small-scale builder) by formulating decision rules. The computerized simulation model provided feedback performance scores which indicated the subject's profit level in response to the decision rules. Motivation of the subjects was reinforced by making their performance in the task part of their student assessments.

The relevant results from Gold's study are that the on-line groups made more 'profit' than the off-line group (a final average of $1444 against $1244, from a starting point of $1000); the on-line group used 20% fewer man-hours, but nearly six times as much computer time; there was a clear preference for the use of the on-line mode.

Gold's study was very useful because it posed a nontrivial open-ended problem for the subjects, that was equally applicable to either the on-line or the off-line mode. The problem also required sustained effort over many hours and the exercise of genuine problem-solving skills, and improved performance was reflected unequivocably in the subject's score. If there is any significant improvement in problem-solving abilities to be expected from man–computer interaction, then Gold's study should have demonstrated it—and it did, but only in terms of on-line versus off-line comparisons.

4.3 Comparison of human and machine performances

The research literature on human–computer interaction is notably sparse. That which does exist is concerned almost exclusively with comparisons of the effectiveness of time-sharing against that of batch-processing systems—we are presumably meant to accept that either of these modes of computer use is better than not using a computer at all. Such a partisan attitude seems hardly acceptable in those areas, such as designing, where the tasks to be accomplished have for centuries been conducted with only rudimentary mechanical aids.

Of course it is difficult and often futile to attempt to compare human and machine abilities in similar tasks, since human and machine attributes are very dissimilar. The tasks which machines are set to perform are therefore not usually tasks which humans excel at, and vice versa. However, we should expect *some* quantitative comparisons to have been made of human performances versus computer performances in order to confirm (or deny) the usually extravagant claims of the computer manufacturers and programmers. In fact, amongst the sparse literature on man–computer studies, human versus machine comparison studies are almost nonexistent.

4.3.1 A queuing problem

A study by Shaffer (1965) evaluated human performance against computer performance in a dynamic problem-solving context in which a continuous sequence of decisions is required in real time. The model used by Shaffer for such a sequential decisionmaking procedure was the problem of serving a queue of randomly arriving customers. Shaffer compared human performance with that of an optimizing service model embodied in a computer program, and found that "subject performance was usually more risky, sometimes more conservative and nearly always more costly (than the computer program). It was seldom optimal."

In a second experiment, designed to evaluate human–computer collaboration, Shaffer arranged for the human subjects to monitor a variety of computer-generated decision sequences on-line. The subjects could alter the computer's decisions in order to achieve better sequences. Shaffer found that, "given optimal solutions, subjects degraded them, given inferior solutions they improved them". The overall conclusion from these experiments therefore is that human performance in this task is generally worse than machine performance, and that man–machine collaboration tends to produce a performance similar to that of unaided humans. Thus there was no sign of 'man–computer symbiosis' producing better results than either man or computer alone.

4.3.2 A building design problem

An experiment to compare computer-aided with unaided approaches to building design problems was conducted by Bazjanac (1972). The task was the design of a high-rise office building, to which the Building Optimization Program (BOP) developed by architects Skidmore, Owings and Merrill could be applied. Two student design teams worked on the same problem independently of each other, one team using BOP extensively as a generative and evaluative tool, the other team using no such aids.

Bazjanac found that "it was not possible to measure any appreciable difference between the two resulting schemes within the context of the real problem, and no definite causalities could be attributed to the use of BOP". Bazjanac suggested that a reason for this ineffectiveness of the computer was that its use requires simplified approximations of design solutions, which make the quantitative results obtained from the computer unreliable.

4.3.3 A travelling salesman problem

These two studies (Shaffer's and Bazjanac's) suggest that there is no advantage to man–machine collaboration in problem solving. However, a different conclusion was reached in a study by Michie et al (1968). This study compared unaided humans with computer-aided humans, and both groups with a heuristic computer program. The problem-solving task was of the 'shortest route' (or 'travelling salesman') type—to find the shortest continuous line connecting a number of scattered points. The 'travelling salesman' problem has attracted the attention of many mathematicians, who have attempted to produce an algorithm for its solution.

Michie et al had a fairly sophisticated heuristic computer program for generating solutions to this type of problem, and they compared solutions generated thus for five fifty-point problems with solutions generated by a group of unaided subjects and with the same group aided by an interactive computer program which calculates the cost (length of line) of any solution or part-solution generated by the user. This man–machine interaction was effected through a cathode-ray-tube graphic display, on which the user could 'draw' and modify his solution with a light pen. They found an average 6% improvement in results obtained by the subjects when using the interactive program, as compared with their unaided attempts. Solutions generated automatically by the heuristic program averaged a further 2% improvement over those of the man–machine combination.

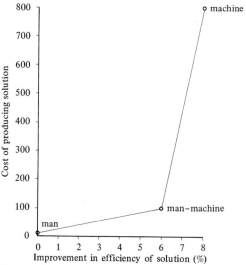

Figure 4.1 The cost and efficiency of different problem-solving modes, according to Michie et al (1968).

Michie et al made a further comparison of the expenses involved in generating solutions in the three modes: man, man–machine, and machine (figure 4.1). They concluded that the man–machine mode is to be preferred for this type of problem, as it produces a 'nontrivial' (6%) improvement in results (compared with unaided humans) for an acceptable rise in expense, whereas the automatic machine results are only marginally further better for a considerable rise in expense. This conclusion confirms the intuitive model generally used to justify the development of interactive computer programs. It would seem, however, to be at variance with the findings of Shaffer and Bazjanac.

These three separate studies are not strictly comparable with each other because they utilize different types of problem, different computer use, etc. They perhaps do demonstrate that the value of computer aids to problem solving is by no means a foregone conclusion, and that considerable further research is required both to justify and (if justified) to refine the application of computer aids.

4.4 A computable design problem
The initial difficulty to be overcome in seeking to obtain performance comparisons between humans and machines in a design context is that of finding a design problem which they may tackle on approximately equal terms. Many such comparisons would, as noted above, be futile since human and machine attributes are very dissimilar. The relevance of establishing performance comparisons here is that one can assess the effectiveness of computer programs which are proposed either as replacements for human problem-solvers, or as aids to human problem-solvers. In either case the programmers' proposals generally assume that the programs will produce, or help produce, better solutions than are obtainable by unaided humans.

The variety of computer applications in architectural design has been reviewed by Maver (1970), who identifies three major categories of models used: formal mathematical models, heuristic models, and simulation models. Formal mathematical modelling includes such techniques as linear programming (for example as applied in computer programs for architectural design by Moseley, 1963; Krejcirik and Sipler, 1965) and cluster analysis (for example Alexander, 1964; Milne, 1970). Heuristic modelling has been applied in those problem areas which are not susceptible to algorithmic solution (for example Whitehead and Eldars, 1965; Willoughby et al, 1970). Simulation programs have been used to model the behaviour of proposed solutions (for example Souder et al, 1964; Negroponte and Groisser, 1970).

As Maver points out, these three types of model correspond to the three principle stages of the design process: analysis, synthesis, and evaluation. However, it is the middle, synthesis, stage at which the crucial creative 'designing' occurs, and it is here also, interestingly, where comparisons of human and machine performance can perhaps most effectively be made. Heuristic modelling is necessary at the synthesis stage because so often there is no *certain* way of achieving an optimum solution to a design problem.

Synthesis problems, therefore, provide a reasonable basis for the comparison of human and machine performance, since the heuristic problem-solving attributes of humans and machines are not so dissimilar as they are in algorithmic problem solving. It would also be constructive to assess the effectiveness of computer programs at the synthesis stage, where they are generally proposed as direct replacements for manual procedures.

4.4.1 Room layouts

The particular synthesis problem most often tackled by computer programmers is that of room layouts or similar spatial arrangements— perhaps the central task of architectural design. To justify computer use, this problem is generally defined as the production of a layout of components (rooms) to be included in the solution such that, given the value for each pair of components of some common relationship parameter for all components, the 'cost' of the layout is minimized. The 'cost' of any layout is measured as $\Sigma d_{ij} A_{ij}$; that is, the sum, for each pair of rooms, of their distance apart multiplied by their association value. Thus, in a good layout, components which have a high association value should be placed close together, whilst those with lower values can be relatively farther apart.

There is no known algorithm for the construction of an optimum solution to such a problem (other than by exhaustively evaluating every possible layout—a procedure which is impossibly lengthy with anything other than a trivially small number of components in the problem). The computer programs which have been written for this problem generate solutions either by a strategy of constructing layouts by placing components one-at-a-time at adjacent locations of a planning grid, starting with the components having highest association values and progressing outwards from the centre of the grid with progressively less strongly associated components, or by taking a given (perhaps random or arbitrary) layout and continually swapping the locations of pairs of rooms to seek cost improvements. The 'swapping of pairs' heuristic has been employed by Buffa et al (1964), Stabler (1967) and others. The 'construction' heuristic has been used by Whitehead and Eldars (1965), Beaumont (1967) and others.

The values for the association parameter most often have been derived from the amount of circulation which is expected to take place between rooms in the completed building. That is, the association value for any pair of rooms is the number of journeys which will be made between those rooms by the building's occupants over some standard time period. Weightings for different types of journey, or journeys by different types of occupant, can be applied to the basic values. Other measures such as social or psychological relationship values, or inverse relationships such as separating noisy from quiet activities, can of course be used instead of, or in addition to, circulation values in determining the desired association patterns.

Whitehead (1970) justifies the use of circulation measures (and such approaches to design) from an analysis of the running costs of an operating theatre suite: "The cost of human movement between rooms was found to be approximately one-third of the total salary cost of staff time, that is, about 23% of the total annual cost of the suite, thus showing the large potential for savings in that sphere and, in default of other equally measurable and important criteria, presenting a strong case for the use of the circulation of people as the prime data in deciding the layout of that type of building".

The spatial-arrangement, or 'room layout', problem was used as the basis for comparisons of human and machine performances in solving design problems in the experiments reported in chapter 5.

The effectiveness of computer aids

5.1 Man versus machine

This chapter is a report of experiments conducted by the author to assess the effectiveness of designers using computer aids in comparison with the effectiveness of unaided designers. The experiments are reported in some detail since they have not been published elsewhere. A pilot study was first conducted to provide a simple comparison of 'man versus machine' abilities to solve problems derived from a design context. The particular problem selected as a basis for this comparison, as explained in the previous chapter, was that of producing a layout of rooms for a building design such that the 'cost' of the layout is minimized.

5.1.1 Experimental design

Task

Seven layout problems with varying numbers of rooms, were designed for the experiment. Four problems involved a layout of six rooms, and the other three problems involved a layout of eight, ten, and twelve rooms, respectively. The problems were arranged in a sequence such that the numbers of rooms per problem were in the order six, eight, six, ten, six, twelve, six. The six-room problems were set alternately with the others so that any learning effect during the course of the experiment could be assessed by reference to the subjects' performance over this set of six-room problems. Essentially, therefore, the pattern of the task was a set of problems of increasing complexity—of six, eight, ten, and twelve rooms—interspersed with further six-room problems, all of a similar complexity.

The 'complexity' of a layout problem is, however, difficult to measure. In addition to the number of rooms, the complexity is determined by the matrix of relationship values of pairs of rooms. If a few pairs of rooms have obviously very high relationship values and all the others have obviously very low relationship values, then the problem is less complex than one in which a pattern of relationships is not immediately visible. The complexity of the problem might also vary with the order of magnitude of the relationship values, since human beings can perhaps more easily compare the relative values of single-digit numbers than, say, triple-digit numbers. In an attempt to overcome these difficulties, and so that the complexity of each problem would be largely determined by the number of rooms required to be located, the matrices of relationship values for the problems were made up from a sequence of single-digit numbers taken from a table of random numbers. As is usual with this type of problem, the relationship matrices were symmetrical about the diagonal—that is, for any pair of rooms i and j, the relationship R_{ij} is the same as the relationship R_{ji}.

One further issue, which also relates to the problems' complexities, remains. That is the freedom with which subjects were allowed to locate rooms within the two-dimensional layout grid. This was closely constrained for the experiment, such that each problem had a defined grid within which all rooms had to be placed, and which had just sufficient grid spaces for the number of rooms. (In these problems a 'room' is an idealized concept and is represented merely by a location in the layout grid.) The layout grid for each problem was rectangular and had an area equal to twice the number of rooms, but the rooms had to be located chequerboard style in alternate grid spaces, not adjacent ones, and hence there was only one location per room. The rule of alternate grid spaces was introduced as a constraint which would make solution of the problem seem more difficult than a simple clustering of the rooms.

Subjects
The subjects used in the experiment were recruited from postgraduate students of design technology at the Design Research Laboratory, University of Manchester Institute of Science and Technology (UMIST). Students of design technology come from a wide range of backgrounds, and include many from architecture. Five subjects volunteered for the experiment: two architects and three nonarchitects. The volunteers were not told beforehand the precise nature of the experiment, only that it was to be an experiment in problemsolving.

Modes of problem solving
There were two experimental modes of solving the set of problems; (1) unaided humans and (2) a computer program for automatically generating solutions to such problems. The human problem solvers were allowed no aids except the use of predrawn grids. The program used to generate 'machine' solutions was derived from programs written as part of some earlier work at the Design Research Laboratory by Stabler (1967). He wrote a suite of programs for a design procedure named CARD (Computer-Aided Room-layout Design), the basis of which is an 'optimization' routine which will attempt to find the lowest-cost layout by swapping the locations of pairs of rooms. The initial locations of the rooms may be either fixed by the designer or randomly decided by another CARD routine. Pairs of rooms to be swapped are selected by the routine at random, and the cost of the layouts compared before and after the swap. If the cost is reduced after the swap, then the new layout is retained; if the cost is not reduced, then the swap is reversed to the previous layout and another pair of rooms is selected for the next attempt.
 This procedure will obviously continue indefinitely unless some limit is set to the number of swaps to be attempted, and in the CARD routine this limit is set by the user. Stabler's recommendation is that the swapping procedure should be terminated when the number of swaps which have been attempted without any further reduction in the layout

cost equals one-quarter times the square of the number of rooms in the layout. Obviously this recommendation is meant to provide a nonlinear function which relates to the nonlinear increase in the number of possible alternative layouts as the number of rooms to be included increases. Stabler does not discuss any rationale for deciding the number of attempted swaps which should be made, and this is a point which will be returned to later.

The full CARD procedure also includes routines for setting constraints, estimating circulation densities between rooms, etc, but this study was concerned with comparing the performance of the 'optimization' routine with human performance in the same task. The 'optimization' method utilized in the CARD routine (that is swapping locations of pairs of rooms) affords particularly interesting comparisons with human performance because it does not always produce exactly the same layout, as some other methods do, and the range of layouts it produces can therefore be compared with the range of layouts produced for the same problem by a number of human subjects. Each particular layout produced by the CARD routine is determined by the sequence of random selections of room pairs for swapping and by the number of swaps attempted.

Procedure

The subjects were given the details of the seven layout problems to be solved, and the procedure for deriving the cost of a layout was explained, but no advice on how to achieve low-cost layouts was given. The time taken by each subject on each problem was recorded.

After a simple four-room training problem to explain the procedure and accustom the subjects to it, each subject worked through the problems at his or her own pace. The subjects only had to produce what they thought were reasonable attempts at finding low-cost solutions. They were not asked to compute the costs of their solutions; this was done later by the experimenter. After completing all seven problems, the subjects were asked to make notes on the procedures they had adopted for solving the problems.

Computer results for the same problems were obtained from the CARD optimization routine, on the University of Manchester Atlas computer. Five solutions to each problem were produced by the routine for comparison with the five subjects' solutions. Sets of five solutions per problem were obtained from each of the three runs of the routine, with the termination point of the routine set at three different values for the number of swaps to be attempted without further improvement of the layout cost. In the first run, this value was set at Stabler's recommended $\frac{1}{4}r^2$; in the second run it was set at $\frac{1}{2}r^2$; and in the third run it was set at r^2, where r is the number of rooms. These different values were tried in order to attempt some assessment of what might be the best value.

5.1.2 Results

Performance measures

The primary measure of performance used for analyzing the results of this experiment was the costs of the layouts produced by the subjects and by the computer routine. 'Cost' was calculated in the manner used by the CARD routine; that is, to determine for each room the sum of the products of its relationship value and its distance to every other room. Distance was calculated as the sum of the difference in both dimensions between the rooms' locations in the planning matrix.

The time taken to produce the layouts has also been considered in some analyses of the results, but this measure cannot be used with any confidence for comparing human and computer performances. The subjects were told not to be concerned with the time they took over the problems, and it is also extremely difficult to add appropriate allowances to the computer time for program writing, data preparation, etc. Time measures do have a limited usefulness in this experiment, however, for assessing any learning effects in the subjects and for comparisons between the three computer runs.

There are some difficulties associated with the type of problem used in this experiment which mean that only fairly simple comparisons can be made of the layout costs achieved by the subjects and by the computer routine. It is not possible, for example, to know whether the costs achieved are approaching the absolute minimum-cost layout. Nor is it possible to know whether it might be relatively easy to produce low-cost layouts for any problem; there may be a large number of layouts which give close, or identical, costs which are fairly low, or there may be very few layouts giving similarly low costs. It is not possible to predict either the range of possible costs (minimum and maximum) for a given problem, or the distribution of costs within that range.

However, it is possible to calculate the *mean* cost of all possible solutions for any given problem, such as those used in this experiment, where the spaces in which rooms may be placed are fixed in number and location. This mean cost is the sum of all the distances between permissible locations multiplied by the sum of all values in the relationship matrix divided by the number of room pairs.[1]

Human performance

Results obtained from the five subjects are given in table 5.1 which shows, for each problem, the mean cost of all possible layouts, the costs achieved by each subject, and the means of the subjects' costs. The times taken by each subject for each problem are also given.

[1] I am indebted to a colleague, R J Talbot, for deriving this formula:

Mean possible solution cost $= \left(\sum d_{ij} \sum A_{ij} \right) \big/ N$, where

d_{ij} is the distance between two locations i and j in the layout,
A_{ij} is the relationship value between room i and room j,
N is the number of relationship pairs in a given problem.

   The subjects are identified as S1, S2, etc in rank order of their overall
mean costs for the seven problems. It can be seen that some subjects
fairly consistently achieved lower costs than other subjects. On the
overall mean costs, the performance range is from 10% to 6% below the
mean of the seven mean costs of all possible layouts. Some subjects were
also consistently quicker than others in completing problems, as can be
seen from the times given in table 5.1, although the quicker subjects did
not necessarily achieve either the higher or the lower costs. Individual
performances will be discussed later.

Table 5.1. Layout costs achieved and times taken by subjects.

Problem number	1	2	3	4	5	6	7	Mean
Number of rooms	6	8	6	10	6	12	6	
Mean cost of all possible layouts	400	674	324	1433	269	1958	339	771
Subjects' costs								
S1	372	612	292	1324	232	1724	304	694
S2	392	616	292	1330	228	1784	304	707
S3	380	620	308	1344	256	1776	320	715
S4	368	648	304	1376	248	1788	308	720
S5	384	620	308	1384	252	1828	300	725
Mean	379	623	301	1352	243	1780	307	712
Subjects' times								
S1	190	360	190	430	180	670	230	
S2	270	750	230	660	160	880	200	
S3	140	290	320	760	400	770	380	
S4	120	230	200	340	140	570	110	
S5	340	380	270	990	290	820	180	
Mean	212	402	242	636	234	742	220	

Machine performance
Table 5.2 gives the results obtained for each problem from five operations
of the CARD routine, thus it gives five attempts at a minimum-cost layout
for comparison with the attempts of the five subjects. Time measures
based on the mean number of 'Atlas instructions' used to produce each
layout are also given in this table. (The number of 'instructions' is a time-
equivalent parameter that was used for costing and supervising jobs run on
the Manchester Atlas computer. 10000 instructions equal approximately
one minute of computer time.)
   Three computer runs were made, each with a different value set for the
number of unsuccessful room swaps to be attempted before termination
in order to evaluate these alternatives. These values were, as explained
earlier, $\frac{1}{4}r^2$, $\frac{1}{2}r^2$, and r^2. It could be expected that, as the number of
attempted swaps increases, the layouts produced would both decrease in

cost, and tend towards the same cost for the same problem. In the limit, with a very high number of attempted swaps permitted, one would expect every layout produced by the computer for the same problem to have the same cost, which could be assumed to be the minimum possible for that problem.

The difficulty lies in deciding a 'trade-off' point at which to set the number of attempted swaps, such that a reasonably low cost is achieved with reasonable certainty without using an unreasonable amount of computer time. This will be discussed in more detail later, but table 5.2 shows that, even with the highest number of attempts permitted here (run 3), the costs achieved were not always consistent. There were also some anomalies: for problem 2 the mean cost achieved in run 2 was higher than that achieved in run 1, and for problem 6 the mean cost achieved in run 3 was higher than that achieved in run 2, even though the

Table 5.2. Layout costs achieved and times taken by computer.

Problem number	1	2	3	4	5	6	7
Number of rooms	6	8	6	10	6	12	6
Mean cost of all possible layouts	400	674	324	1433	269	1958	339
Computer's costs Run 1	356	560	300	1276	236	1636	292
	360	564	300	1288	252	1640	304
	364	580	300	1292	252	1656	304
	388	604	300	1296	256	1700	308
	388	620	304	1304	260	1708	308
Mean	371	586	301	1291	251	1668	303
Computer's costs Run 2	356	552	292	1268	228	1616	288
	356	564	300	1272	228	1632	292
	356	596	300	1288	240	1640	304
	364	628	304	1292	256	1648	304
	364	628	304	1304	260	1692	320
Mean	359	594	300	1285	242	1646	302
Computer's costs Run 3	356	552	292	1268	228	1636	288
	356	564	292	1268	228	1640	288
	356	568	292	1276	228	1656	304
	356	584	304	1284	228	1692	304
	364	588	304	1288	228	1700	304
Mean	358	571	297	1277	228	1665	298
Computer's times (mean number of Atlas instructions) Run 1	64	95	66	133	61	226	66
Run 2	83	118	74	220	74	363	78
Run 3	100	177	102	263	97	451	103

mean costs were expected to decrease with each run. Also, in run 2 two
of the costs achieved for problem 6 were lower than any achieved for the
same problem in run 3. These anomalies resulted from the particular
sequence of random selections of room pairs generated in the computer
routine.

Performance comparisons
The layout costs achieved by the subjects and by the three runs of the
computer routine for problems 1, 2, 4, and 6, provide a comparison of
performances on the set of problems of increasing conplexity. In most
cases the computer runs produced significantly better results than the
subjects did; the only cases of doubt were those in which the range of
computer results overlapped the subjects' range. This occurred in computer
run 1 of problem 1 and in runs 1 and 2 of problem 2. The Mann–Whitney
U-test of statistical significance showed that the computer performances
which were *not* significantly better than the subjects' corresponding
performances were run 1 of problem 1, and run 2 of problem 2 ($p = 0 \cdot 21$
in both cases; $p = 0 \cdot 03$ for run 1 of problem 2). The computer routine
termination values set for runs 1 and 2 cannot, therefore, reasonably
guarantee a significantly better set of results than is achievable by human
beings for problems of a complexity up to eight rooms. This is confirmed
by the results from problems 3, 5, and 7 (the other six-room problems), in
all of which computer runs 1 and 2 did not produce results significantly
better than those of the subjects.

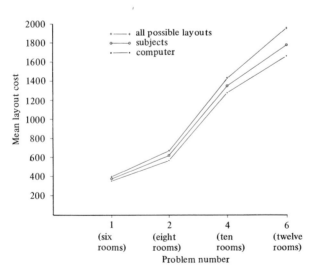

Figure 5.1. The mean costs of all possible layouts, mean costs achieved by subjects,
and mean costs achieved by computer run 3 on problems 1,2,4, and 6.

For problems of higher complexity (more than eight rooms) any of the termination values used in the three computer runs produced significantly better results than were achievable by the human subjects, and in general there did not appear to be any significant differences between the results achieved by the different computer runs, except in problem 4, where run 3 was significantly better than run 1.

Figure 5.1 compares, for problems 1, 2, 4, and 6, the mean layout costs achieved by the subjects with those achieved in computer run 3 and with the mean cost of all possible layouts for the problem. In each problem the subjects' mean cost falls fairly consistently approximately midway between the computer's mean cost and the mean cost of all possible layouts. The average reduction from the mean cost of all possible layouts is approximately 7% for the subjects and 13% for the computer (run 3). In the set of six-room problems the subjects' mean costs are generally much closer to those of the computer.

Figure 5.1 suggests that there may be consistent relationships between the mean cost of all possible layouts for a problem and the mean costs achievable by the subjects and by the computer. This is borne out by figure 5.2 which plots, for problems 1, 2, 4, and 6, the mean costs achieved by subjects and computer against the mean cost of all possible layouts. Best straight lines both for the computer and for the subjects were calculated and can be seen to provide close fits to the points on the graph. Hence there is no indication either of relatively improving or worsening performance by the subjects or by the computer as the mean cost of all possible layouts increases. The mean cost of all possible layouts may therefore be a useful indicator of the relative difficulty of a problem.

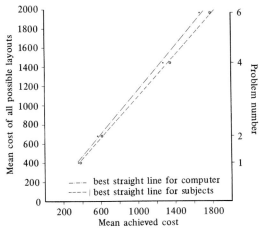

Figure 5.2. The mean costs of all possible layouts versus the mean costs achieved by the subjects and computer run 3.

The difficulty of trying to compare the times taken by subjects and by computer on the problems has already been discussed. Figures 5.3 and 5.4 can be used to compare human and machine time performances only in terms of relative patterns of increase in time with increasing problem complexity. By using mean achieved costs as the measure of complexity, we can see that the subjects tended not to spend directly increasing amounts of time on increasingly difficult problems; rather, their curve flattens as it grows higher.

Since, however, the subjects' performance in terms of costs achieved did increase linearly with increasing problem complexity, we can conclude that they must have improved their efficiency in dealing with the problems of higher complexity. The reverse was true of the computer's times, which showed accelerating curves (figure 5.4). This is as should be expected, since the termination time depended on the square of the number of rooms per problem—a nonlinear function. We can also compare in figure 5.4 the times

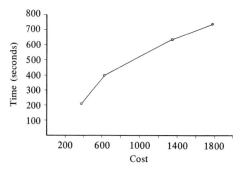

Figure 5.3. The mean time taken per problem by subjects versus their mean costs achieved on problems 1,2,4, and 6.

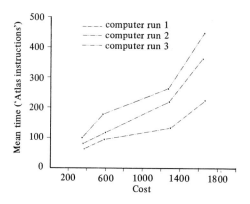

Figure 5.4. The mean time (number of 'Atlas instructions') taken per problem by the computer versus its mean costs achieved on problems 1,2,4, and 6.

taken by the three different computer runs and observe that there is generally a doubling in time between runs 1 and 3, which is possibly not always justified by the relatively small improvements in layout costs obtained with the longer running time.

Individual performances

It has already been noted that some subjects consistently achieved lower layout costs than others, and that some were consistently quicker than others. Figure 5.5 plots for each subject the achieved layout cost against the time taken, for problems 1, 2, 4, and 6. The differences in time taken are very large—over 300% for some problems. These differences between subjects are not particularly important in themselves, but the patterns of time spent by the subjects can be used to assess whether any learning was evident during the experiment.

If there had been either consistent or no learning during the experiment, we would expect consistently varying curves for time against difficulty. Such consistency was exhibited by subjects S1 and S4, whose time curves resemble those of the computer (figure 5.4) and therefore imply that no learning took place in these subjects. Subject S2 was too erratic for any conclusions to be drawn. Subjects S3 and S5 showed consistent time increases over problems 1, 2, and 4, suggesting also that no learning was taking place, but then both showed relatively dramatic improvements on problem 6.

The set of six-room problems, 1, 3, 5, and 7 were placed alternately with the other problems in the task specifically to gain some insight into the subjects' learning patterns. We can see from table 5.1 that, although the mean time per problem in this set remained fairly constant at around 230 seconds, there were considerable differences between subjects. S3 showed a fairly consistent increase in time per problem, whereas S5 and

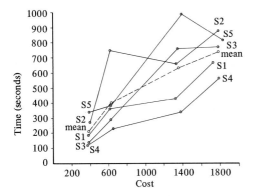

Figure 5.5. The time taken per problem by individual subjects versus their achieved layout costs on problems 1,2,4, and 6.

S2 showed fairly consistent decreases in time per problem. Subjects would be expected to decrease their times per problem over these problems, which were of approximately equal difficulty, if they were learning during the experiment, and indeed this would have been the case for the subjects as a group if it had not been for the abnormal behaviour of S3. The variation in individual times therefore precludes any possibility of inferring that the subjects as a group exhibited any consistent learning effects during the experiment.

Another performance measure, however, was used to look for learning patterns over problems 1, 3, 5, and 7 (figure 5.6). The layout costs achieved by each subject were plotted as a percentage improvement over the mean cost of all possible layouts per problem. Again, there were considerable differences between subjects, but the general trend was an increase in the percentage improvement, suggesting that the subjects were generally improving their performances during the experiment.

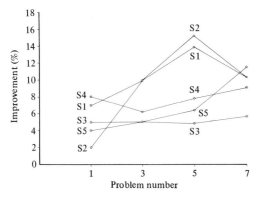

Figure 5.6. The percentage improvement over the mean cost of all possible layouts, as achieved by each subject on problems 1,3,5, and 7.

5.1.3 Discussion
Experimental design
There are some obvious shortcomings in the design of the experiment which must be borne in mind when attempting to interpret the results. Firstly, there were few subjects, and they were entirely unrepresentative of any group except themselves. Secondly, the subjects used whatever intuitive strategies they might for solving the problems, whereas the computer routine used one specific procedure, and other computer routines which use different procedures for solving this kind of problem might well produce different results.

The final, and perhaps major, reservation which must be expressed is whether any relevant comparison can be made between the problems used in this experiment and 'real world' problems. This is a criticism which can readily be made of the attempts to write computer programs to solve architectural design problems—the simplifications which have to be imposed on the problems in order to make them amenable to computer solution often remove any usefulness from the programs. Certainly in this experiment the problems were highly constrained to suit the capabilities of the computer program; the real-world problems they were meant to model are much more complicated. This does not remove all value from the experiment, but it must be remembered that the computer was very definitely playing on its home ground, and only very limited conclusions on man and machine problem-solving abilities can be made.

Results
We have seen that, for problems of the type in this experiment, the solutions produced by human subjects and by the computer were not significantly different in cost for problems of up to eight rooms, unless the highest computer termination value (run 3) was used. Since the subjects generally took less than seven minutes to solve the eight-room problem, it would seem that it is not worth the data preparation, etc, and computer time involved in obtaining computer solutions to problems of this size. For larger problems the computer solutions became increasingly better than the humans', even with a low termination value for the computer routine. It is very difficult to make any generalized economic comparisons between man and machine, however, unless we have some measure of a 'true' cost which is likely to be saved in the final design by a reduction in the theoretical layout cost, and which can be used in a trade-off against the respective times and costs involved in obtaining solutions by man and by machine.

There were also large differences in the performances of individual subjects, which often precluded discussion of their performance as a group. There did appear to be some learning during the experiment, particularly in terms of improving the percentage reduction from the mean cost of all possible layouts, and so perhaps with practice in this kind of problem solving we might expect human abilities to improve.

5.2 Man versus man–machine versus machine

The objective of the next set of experiments was to enable performance comparisons to be made for the same design task as accomplished by (1) unaided humans, (2) humans working with an appropriate interactive computer aid, and (3) typical computer programs for automatically generating solutions for the particular task.

5.2.1 Experimental design
Task
The design task chosen for the experiment was the arrangement of a given set of twelve rectangular 'rooms' (of three different but fixed shapes) to a minimum cost as determined by a given matrix of relationship values.

D

The details of the task were based on a hospital-layout problem used by Whitehead and Eldars (1965) as a demonstration of their program for generating a solution to such a problem. Twenty-one rooms were included in the original problem as reported by Whitehead and Eldars, but here the problem was simplified to a set of twelve most strongly interrelated rooms. Figure 5.7 presents the interaction matrix of relationship values used in the experiment.

This task therefore contained the same number of rooms to be arranged as in the largest problem of the previous (man versus machine) experiment. However, in this case the problem was more complex because (1) the relationship values in the interaction matrix covered a much wider absolute range (1 to 182), (2) the rooms were of varying sizes, and (3) the base grid for locating the rooms in a layout did not constrain the rooms to any particular set of locations. The base grid for arranging layouts in this task was in fact merely a relatively large grid of available empty squares.

Subjects

This set of experiments was carried out with the assistance of the Department of Architecture and Building Science of the University of Strathclyde, Glasgow. The subjects were twelve volunteers from the second and third undergraduate years of the department, there being six volunteers from each of the two years.

room number	1	2	3	4	5	6	7	8	9	10	11	12
1		7	23	40	1	1	23	128	40	23	7	181
2			56	9	24	16	52	113	9	8	62	11
3				85	7	4	13	51	39	56	8	21
4					123	123	111	111	32	39	9	3
5						151	22	20	123	7	24	1
6							16	13	123	4	16	3
7								182	111	13	52	8
8									111	51	113	106
9										85	9	3
10											56	21
11												11
12												

Figure 5.7. Problem interaction matrix used for the man versus man–machine versus machine experiments.

Modes of problem solving

Basically there were three experimental modes: unaided humans, humans aided by an appropriate interactive computer program, and automatically generated computer solutions. However, within the 'unaided human' mode a subdivision was made into humans attempting to solve the problem entirely intuitively and humans using a fixed strategy. The strategy given was that of attempting to work to the solution strategy used by the Whitehead and Eldars' program—placing the most strongly related pair of rooms first, then the room most strongly related to that pair, and so on. Obviously this strategy eventually needs mechanical aid of some kind to handle the necessary computations, but it was hypothesized that some such conscious strategy might improve the results obtained by the subjects.

The interactive computer program used for the man–machine mode was part of a larger design evaluation program, and was generously made available for these experiments by the Architecture and Building Aids Computer Unit, Strathclyde. This program requires the designer to specify his design solution to the computer (through an on-line teletype terminal). The program then replies with the 'cost' of the layout (using the previously stored relationship matrix) plus a table of data which indicate the degree to which the desired proximities of components (as determined by the relationshp values) have been achieved. Briefly these data are intended to show whether each pair of components is relatively too far apart or relatively too close to each other in the proposed solution, calculated as follows:

If the relationship value between components i and j is A_{ij} and the distance between these components in the proposed solution is d_{ij}, then ideally A_{ij} should be inversely proportional to d_{ij}—that is, the greater the relationship between two components the closer together they should be. In other words, ideally $d_{ij}A_{ij} = K$, a constant. Since the magnitude of this constant will vary from problem to problem depending on the problem size and the scale of relationship values, a standardization is performed by computing the set of values

$$\frac{d_{ij}A_{ij} - \overline{d_{ij}A_{ij}}}{\overline{d_{ij}A_{ij}}},$$

where $\overline{d_{ij}A_{ij}}$ is the mean value of $d_{ij}A_{ij}$, and these are printed out in matrix form. Since the ideal situation is represented by zero values in the matrix, it follows that a high positive value for any pair of components would indicate that these two components have been located too far apart; a high negative value would indicate that the two components have been located too close together relative to the overall pattern of locations.

The program then asks if the user wishes to modify his proposed solution. If so, the user types in whatever modifications he wishes to make and the program responds with the cost of this new layout, and the revised matrix of relative-location data. The intention, of course, is that the user should be able to assess, from the matrix of relative-location data, which components he has placed too far apart (or unnecessarily close together), modify his solution accordingly, and once again seek the computer program's advice. Working in this iterative fashion, the designer should be able to move progressively towards a lower-cost solution. A hypothetical example of using the layout evaluation program in this way is shown in figure 5.8.

```
SIGMA AD =      7527.66
        1      2      3      4      5      6      7      8      9     10     11
2    -.91
3    -.70   0.47
4    -.26   -.74   0.12
5    -.97   -.23   -.75   2.05
6    -.96   -.50   -.83   3.35   0.99
7    -.58   0.02   -.68   1.01   -.71   -.70
8    0.25   0.40   -.00   1.01   -.56   -.67   0.60
9    0.02   -.86   0.46   0.12   2.05   1.22   1.01   1.01
10   -.07   -.73   1.80   0.68   -.85   -.96   -.67   0.58   0.54
11   -.87   -.18   -.76   -.67   0.07   -.30   0.66   1.67   -.75   1.56
12   0.59   -.83   -.67   -.92   -.96   -.87   -.79   0.92   -.91   -.00   -.85

DO YOU WISH TO ALTER GEOMETRICAL INPUT      0/1
 ?

 1

TYPE COMPONENT NO. ON ONE LINE
AND ON NEXT LINE 4 COORDINATES
COMPONENT NO.
 ?10

COORDINATES
 ?4,9,5,9

COMPONENT NO.
 ?0

SIGMA AD =      7171.45
        1      2      3      4      5      6      7      8      9     10     11
2    -.90
3    -.68   0.55
4    -.22   -.72   0.17
5    -.97   -.20   -.74   2.20
6    -.96   -.48   -.82   3.56   1.08
7    -.56   0.07   -.66   1.11   -.70   -.69
8    0.32   0.47   0.05   1.11   -.54   -.65   0.67
9    0.07   -.85   0.53   0.18   2.20   1.33   1.11   1.11
10   -.36   -.88   1.33   0.77   -.70   -.85   -.58   0.37   0.61
11   -.86   -.14   -.75   -.65   0.13   -.26   0-74   1.80   -.74   0.02
12   0.67   -.82   -.65   -.92   -.96   -.86   -.78   1.01   -.90   -.41   -.84

DO YOU WISH TO ALTER GEOMETRICAL INPUT?      0/1
 ?
```

Figure 5.8. Part of a typical run of the evaluation program. After the user has input coordinates of the complete layout, he can change the position of individual rooms (components) by redefining coordinates so as to achieve a layout of lower cost (sigma AD).

The automatic machine mode of problem solving for the experiment was to obtain solutions to the problem from (1) the Whitehead and Eldars' (1964, 1965) approach, and (2) the STUNI program (Willoughby et al, 1970).

Procedure
In the first stage of the set of experiments, the subjects were informed of the objective of the layout problem—to achieve minimum-cost layouts. The number and shapes of 'rooms' to be located, and the purpose and details of the interaction matrix of relationship values were described. To familiarize the subjects with the particular problem, each was given a set of cardboard rectangles representing the twelve components to be placed and was asked to attempt a minimum-cost layout using these cardboard models. Only ten minutes were allowed for this first attempt, which was used to obtain a set of initial performance scores for comparison with later, lengthier attempts. The cardboard models were not used in the subsequent attempts.

The subjects were then divided into three groups of four, two students from each of the two years being randomly assigned to each of the groups. These groups were then separately conducted through the subsequent stages of experiments, thus:

Group 1 subjects were asked to make further attempts at obtaining a minimum-cost layout, with no further assistance of any kind.

Group 2 subjects first had explained to them the strategy of building up layouts by starting with the most strongly related pair, etc, and then were asked to follow a similar strategy as far as possible in making further attempts at obtaining a minimum-cost layout.
These subjects were asked to follow a similar strategy as far as possible.

Group 3 subjects were familiarized with the use of the layout evaluation program at a computer terminal, and asked to use this program to help them achieve a minimum-cost layout.

All subjects were allowed up to one hour for this stage of their involvement in the experiments. All except one subject (in group 3) used the full hour allowed. Subsequently the Whitehead and Eldars solution and the STUNI solution costs were calculated in order to provide the 'machine' performance measures.

5.2.2 Results
Human performance
The results obtained are detailed in table 5.3. As was to be expected, the scatter of individual scores for their initial attempts at the problem showed no systematic bias towards any of the three groups the subjects were later divided into. Although the mean scores of the subjects, when allocated to groups, do rank in group order, this is entirely fortuitous.

As can be seen from the final scores in table 5.3, all unaided subjects improved on their initial scores, whereas this is not true of the other two groups. In the placement-strategy group, two subjects improved on their initial scores, and in the group using the computer evaluation program only one subject improved on his initial score.

Table 5.3. Attempts at obtaining a minimum-cost room layout under different conditions. Group 1 subjects were unaided, group 2 subjects were given a strategy, and group 3 subjects used an interactive computer program.

Subject	Initial scores			Final scores		
	group 1	group 2	group 3	group 1	group 2	group 3
A	8065	7617	7914	8017	6949	7515
B	7494	7123	7366	7133	7899	7914
C	7483	7603	7352	7464	7626	8649
D	8201	8297	7515	7420	7223	7828
Mean	7811	7660	7537	7509	7424	7977

Man–machine performance
In group 3 the final mean score was higher (that is, performance was worse) than the initial mean score for that group. Table 5.4 shows the sets of consecutive scores achieved by each subject in this group as they attempted to improve their solutions, using the evaluative computer program output as a guide. The only subject in this group whose final score was better than his initial score [subject 3(A), who was also the one not to use the full hour allotted] achieved this improvement with his first modification, and then decided it would not be possible to improve further. For all other subjects in this group, most of their consecutive modifications produced results which were worse, instead of better, than the preceding attempt. (Note that, for groups 1 and 2, consecutive attempts were not recorded; each subject was asked only to produce a final solution which he thought would be better than his initial attempt.)

Table 5.4. Consecutive attempts by subjects in group 3.

Subject	Attempt				
	initial	1	2	3	4
A	7914	7515			
B	7366	7516	7422	7486	7914
C	7352	7553	8216	8649	
D	7515	7868	7975	7828	

Machine performance
The two 'machine' solutions to the given problem were evaluated with the same program as was used for computing the scores of the subjects' solutions. The resulting scores were:

Whitehead and Eldars program   7752,
STUNI program   7810,
Mean   7781.

Performance comparisons
Figure 5.9 is a composite graph showing the initial and final scores of each subject, the mean initial score, and the mean final score of each group, and the scores of the two 'machine' solutions.

    The 'machine' scores were close to the mean initial score of the subjects (7669). The mean final score of group 1 (unaided) was 3·5% better than the mean 'machine' score. The best mean final score of any of the groups (group 2—placement-strategy) was an improvement of approximately 4·5% over the 'machine' solutions. The *best* individual score, 6949 by subject 2(A), was approximately 11% better than the mean score of the two 'machine' solutions. The *worst* individual score, 8649 by subject 3(C), was approximately 11% worse than the mean score of the two 'machine' solutions, and the mean final score of group 3 ('man–machine') was slightly worse than the 'machine' solutions.

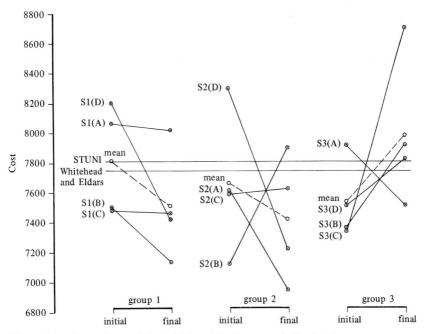

Figure 5.9. Comparisons of the initial and final scores of all subjects.

If performance improvements are compared between groups, group 1 made an overall improvement from initial to final mean scores of 3·9%, and group 2 made an overall improvement of 3·1%. Group 3's final mean score was 5·8% *worse* than its mean initial score.

Within the groups, individual performances varied widely, from an improvement of 13% [subject 2(D)] to a worsening of 17·7% [subject 3(C)]. All members of group 1 improved their scores, whereas in group 2 two subjects improved and two worsened their score. All except one member of group 3 worsened their scores between initial and final attempts.

5.2.3 Discussion
Experimental design

A number of details in the design of this experiment were influenced by the earlier, 'man versus machine' experiment. The subjects for example were chosen as far as possible as a homogeneous group, so as to minimize differences in individual abilities. Although the volunteers were self-selected for participation in these experiments, there is no reason to believe that the twelve subjects were not representative of second and third year undergraduate architectural students—that is, approximately halfway through their professional training. The task to be attempted by the subjects had the same number of 'rooms' (twelve) as the largest problem of the earlier experiment, where significant differences in human and machine performances became clear. However, in these later experiments the problem was more complex than the earlier twelve-room problem in that the 'rooms' were of varying sizes, the interaction relationship values fell in a much wider absolute range, and the solution space was much less constrained. In these respects, this problem is more representative of 'real world' design problems.

One further detail of the experimental design was the use of two 'manual' groups—the completely unaided group 1 and the use of a particular strategy in group 2. This detail was introduced as an attempt to assess the competence of humans relative to that of machines when they are using a similar heuristic to solve the problem, and to see if such a fixed strategy was any aid to human problem solvers.

Results

Given the apparent greater 'size' of problem used in this set of experiments compared with the size of problems in the earlier 'man versus machine' experiment, it could be expected that the machine results would be superior to the humans' results. However, such a prediction would be dubious because the computer programs necessary for this more complex type of problem use a different heuristic from that suitable for the simpler problems. In the event the results show that the Whitehead and Eldars and STUNI programs produced results very close to each other and approximately in the middle of the range of scatter of the humans' initial results. Since these initial results were quick (ten-minute) familiarization attempts by the subjects, it is clear that the computer programs do not justify themselves on problems of this size. If any parallels can be drawn from the earlier experiment comparing man with machine, then it must be assumed that a clear divergence of human and machine abilities at solving this more complex type of problem would only become evident with problems of approximately double the size of the one used here. Even then this is in terms of a comparison with quick, initial solution attempts by humans. After they had been allowed a further one hour to improve their solutions, three of the four 'unaided' subjects (group 1) produced better results than the computer programs had done. The mean final score of group 1 was 3·5% better than the mean of the two 'machine' scores.

It is difficult to assess the value of using the placement strategy. Although two subjects in this group made significant improvements in their final solutions as compared with their initial ones [8·8% and 13% for subjects 2(A) and 2(D) respectively], one became slightly worse and the other [subject 2(B)] produced a marked worsening (10·9%). However, the mean final score of group 2 was the lowest of all the groups, although no subjects in group 1 produced final results worse than their initial ones (improvements being 0·6%, 4·8%, 0·25%, and 9·5%) and the mean improvement was higher for group 1 (3·9%) than it was for group 2 (3·1%). It seems, therefore, that no definite assistance could generally be claimed for the use of the placement strategy, and that in some cases it could even be unhelpful.

The most striking observation to be made from the results is the adverse effect on performance apparently caused by using the evaluative computer program. In the 'man–machine' group only one subject was able to improve on his initial attempt, and even that was by using the program very conservatively and making only one set of modifications to his initial solution. Such a conservative use of the program would not in itself be a criticism if the program output had conclusively suggested that the particular solution was a relatively well-balanced layout, difficult to improve upon. In this case this was not the situation however, as the program output did indicate certain relatively poor component locations. Obviously the subject was not confident that he could successfully modify his solution further, despite lengthy consideration.

This conservative use of a program that is intended to be used 'interactively' was common to all subjects in this group. The other three subjects in the group made only three or four solution modifications (table 5.4), which indicates a considerable 'thinking time' of fifteen to twenty minutes between interactions with the program. It would seem that either this type of problem is too complex for rapid interaction to occur (that is, the problem requires long periods of thinking time in which to juggle with the solution), or the program itself is not conducive to rapid interaction.

D*

The adverse effect on performance of using this program is evidenced by the fact that solutions produced by group 3 subjects generally became progressively worse as they interacted with the program. Of the eleven modified attempts made by the subjects in this group, only three produced better scores than in the immediately preceding attempt. This is such a remarkably bad performance as to make one wonder whether the program output was not deliberately misleading in some way. However, this does not appear to be the case, as far as can be judged from the details of each subject's sequence of attempts (figures 5.10–5.13).

It is very difficult to deduce how the subjects were responding to the evaluative data output from the program, but perhaps a general error seems to have been to try to concentrate on improving subsolutions to the problem, at the expense of the overall solution. If this is true, then perhaps the program output was in a sense misleading if it seemed to suggest that the relative locations of certain pairs of components needed to be attended to in the solution, whereas other patterns of the solution could be disregarded. In fact the user has to juggle with the total solution pattern continually.

In general it seems probable that the computer program may have been generating more information than could be used effectively (since the subjects had to integrate the evaluative data from the program *and* from the original interaction matrix of relationship values in order to assess what modifications to make), and possibly too 'raw' a form of information.

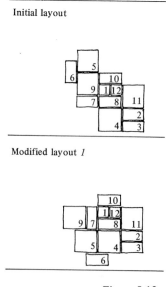

Initial layout

Modified layout *1*

Figure 5.10.

The difficulty subjects had in dealing with the information was indicated by the long 'thinking time' between each interaction with the program.

The overall conclusion which is evident from these results is that, given this type and size of problem, the best performances will be achieved by humans who are left to tackle the problem in their individual ways. This finding is contrary to that of Michie et al (1968) in their study of man versus man–machine versus machine problem solving, and it is therefore necessary to attempt some assessment of the reasons for this difference.

Firstly, the experimental tasks in this study and the Michie study are not the same, and some differences in results could therefore be attributable to that. Secondly, the 'machine' solutions to the shortest-route problems which Michie et al used as the experimental task were derived from programs which have benefited from considerable investment of intellectual effort over the many years for which this type of problem has been a 'classic' for problem solvers; comparable intellectual effort has not yet been devoted to the room-layout problem-solving programs. Thirdly, the 'man–machine' mode used by Michie et al, although it is a fairly minimal computational aid, used a light pen and CRT graphic display which is probably a distinctly advantageous man–machine interface in comparison with the teletype terminal.

The findings of this study are, however, similar to those of Bazjanac (1972), who found no particular advantages for the use of computer aids in the solving of a building design problem.

```
SIGMA AD =        7914.05
        1        2        3        4        5        6        7        8        9       10       11
 2    -.81
 3    -.25    -.53
 4    -.15    -.85    0.46
 5    -.98    0.21    -.60    4.52
 6    -.97    -.13    -.76    4.45    1.27
 7    -.65    0.79    -.52    1.31    -.36    -.61
 8    0.19    1.11    0.20    0.39    -.33    -.53    2.04
 9    -.47    -.65    0.73    -.04    1.05    0.85    0.39    1.31
10    -.79    -.76    1.09    0.14    -.85    -.88    -.69    -.15    0.46
11    -.85    -."2    -.83    -.79    0.00    -.22    0.75    0.94    -.69    0.17
12    0.51    -.77    -.41    -.94    -.97    -.89    -.82    -.01    -.94    -.80    -.85
SIGMA AD =        7515.36
        1        2        3        4        5        6        7        8        9       10       11
 2    -.80
 3    -.21    -.51
 4    -.10    -.84    0.54
 5    -.97    -.15    -.75    1.16
 6    -.96    -.49    -.89    0.95    1.39
 7    -.77    0.74    -.51    1.44    -.60    -.50
 8    0.26    1.22    0.27    0.46    -.56    -.64    1.53
 9    0.07    -.55    1.07    0.13    1.70    3.65    0.95    2.45
10   -.77    -.75    1.20    0.20    -.75    -.82    -.76    -.10    1.84
11    -.84    -.18    -.82    -.78    -.06    -.35    0.60    1.05    -.57    0.23
12    0.59    -.76    -.38    -.93    -.97    -.89    -.86    0.04    -.89    -.79    -.85
```

The sequence of layout modifications made by subject A in group 3 and the computer's evaluation data for each layout.

Initial layout

Modified layout *1*

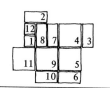

Modified layout *2*

Modified layout *3*

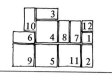

Modified layout *4*

Figure 5.11.

```
SIGMA AD =      7366.37
     1       2       3       4       5       6       7       8       9      10      11
 2  -.93
 3  -.37   0.77
 4   0.27  -.64   3.05
 5  -.97   0.06   -.73   1.20
 6  -.96   -.18   -.86   2.86   1.03
 7  -.58   0.40   -.50   0.49   -.51   -.45
 8   0.28   1.02   0.74   1.49   -.43   -.50   0.63
 9  -.24   -.74   -.13   -.19   1-20   1.76   1.05   1.05
10  -.31   -.69   0.00   0.41   -.84   -.93   -.59   0-62   0.14
11  -.90   0.15   -.89   -.64   -.14   -.39   0.49   1.53   -.84   0.25
12   0.62   -.89   -.24   -.90   -.96   -.86   -.85   0.06   -.92   -.20   -.75
```

```
SIGMA AD =      7516.07
     1       2       3       4       5       6       7       8       9      10      11
 2  -.93
 3   0.01   1.95
 4   0.24   -.64   0.12
 5  -.97   0.04   -.85   1.16
 6  -.95   -.11   -.93   1.70   0.99
 7  -.58   0.37   -.66   0.46   -.52   -.49
 8   0.26   0.98   0.79   1.44   -.44   -.49   0.60
 9  -.25   -.75   0.38   -.21   1.16   2.78   1.01   1.01
10  -.32   -.70   1.43   0.38   -.85   -.87   -.60   0.58   0.12
11  -.90   0.12   -.59   -.65   -.16   -.23   0.46   1.48   -.84   0.23
12   0.59   -.89   -.07   -.91   -.96   -.85   -.86   0.04   -.92   -.21   -.75
```

```
SIGMA AD =      7421.64
     1       2       3       4       5       6       7       8       9      10      11
 2  -.87
 3   0.03   1.36
 4   0.26   -.73   0.13
 5  -.97   -.02   -.84   1.19
 6  -.96   -.17   -.86   2.83   1.01
 7  -.58   -.02   -.65   0.48   -.51   -.46
 8   0.27   0.59   0.81   1.47   -.43   -.50   0.62
 9  -.25   -.71   0.40   -.20   1.19   1.73   1.03   1.03
10  -.31   -.64   1.46   0.40   -.84   -.93   -.59   0.60   0.13
11  -.90   1.01   -.58   -.64   -.15   -.39   0.48   1.51   -.84   0.25
12   0.61   -.89   -.06   -.91   -.96   -.86   -.85   0.05   -.92   -.20   -.75
```

```
SIGMA AD =      7486.02
     1       2       3       4       5       6       7       8       9      10      11
 2  -.93
 3   0.02   1.96
 4   0.25   -.64   0.12
 5  -.97   0.04   -.85   1.17
 6  -.96   -.20   -.87   2.80   1.00
 7  -.58   0.38   -.66   0.47   -.52   -.46
 8   0.26   0.99   0.80   1.45   -.44   -.51   0.60
 9  -.25   -.75   0.39   -.20   1.27   1.71   1.02   1.02
10  -.32   -.70   1.44   0.39   -.85   -.93   -.59   0.59   0.12
11  -.90   0.13   -.59   -.65   -.15   -.40   0.47   1.49   -.84   0.23
12   0.60   -.89   -.07   -.91   -.96   -.86   -.85   0.04   -.92   -.21   -.75
```

```
SIGMA AD =      7914.02
     1       2       3       4       5       6       7       8       9      10      11
 2  -.91
 3  -.23   1.31
 4   0.18   -.70   0.06
 5  -.97   -.30   -.80   1.05
 6  -.95   -.24   -.91   1.11   2.15
 7  -.79   -.03   -.68   1.31   -.41   -.40
 8   1.20   1.67   -.10   0.39   -.58   -.62   0.52
 9   0.90   -.59   0.31   -.25   1.05   0.54   3.56   2.73
10   0.00   -.61   -.26   -.41   -.80   -.95   -.55   0.34   1.16
11  -.88   -.22   -.73   -.79   -.60   -.43   -.11   0.94   -.70   1.15
12   0.51   -.77   -.36   -.91   -.96   -.86   -.93   0.82   -.85   -.12   -.73
```

The sequence of layout modifications made by subject B in group 3 and the computer's evaluation data for each layout.

Initial layout

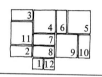

Modified layout *1*

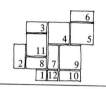

Modified layout *2*

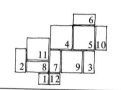

Modified layout *3*

Figure 5.12.

SIGMA AD =   7352.16

	1	2	3	4	5	6	7	8	9	10	11
2	-.89										
3	-.12	0.51									
4	0.27	-.74	0.57								
5	-.96	0.20	-.68	2.31							
6	-.96	-.38	-.87	0.66	1.03						
7	-.57	0.04	-.67	0.49	-.34	-.70					
8	0.28	1.03	0.65	1.49	-.30	-.66	0.63				
9	0.05	-.67	0.65	-.19	1.47	1.28	1.05	1.05			
10	-.12	-.60	2.04	0.41	-.87	-.90	-.59	0.62	0.14		
11	-.82	-.17	-.89	-.82	0.10	-.48	-.04	1.54	-.67	1.81	
12	0.62	-.73	-.11	-.90	-.96	-.90	-.85	0.06	-.94	-.37	-.65

SIGMA AD =   7553.43

	1	2	3	4	5	6	7	8	9	10	11
2	-.85										
3	-.19	0.43									
4	0.33	-.68	0.53								
5	-.96	0.23	-.75	1.15							
6	-.95	-.09	-.86	1.69	0.98						
7	-.64	0.36	-.67	1.00	-.38	-.40					
8	0.25	0.56	0.34	2.11	-.18	-.36	1.51				
9	0.02	-.65	0.33	-.37	1.40	2.91	0.45	1.95			
10	-.50	-.67	1.45	0.24	-.78	-.82	-.76	0.41	0.11		
11	-.84	-.02	-.90	-.82	-.14	-.34	-.18	0.48	-.75	0.91	
12	0.58	-.68	-.22	-.91	-.96	-.85	-.90	0.67	-.94	-.72	-.72

SIGMA AD =   8215.83

	1	2	3	4	5	6	7	8	9	10	11
2	-.86										
3	-.21	1.70									
4	0.22	-.71	1.19								
5	-.96	0.13	-.88	0.98							
6	-.95	- 16	- 89	1.47	0.82						
7	-.67	0.25	-.69	0.84	-.43	-.45					
8	0.15	0.44	0.85	1.85	-.24	-.41	1.31				
9	-.06	-.67	-.53	-.43	1.21	2.60	0.34	1.71			
10	0.13	-.53	0.01	0.10	-.92	-.93	-.53	1.48	1.19		
11	-.86	-.10	-.70	-.84	-.21	-.39	-.25	0.36	-.77	1.51	
12	0.45	-.70	-.43	-.91	-.97	-.87	-.90	0.54	-.95	-.10	-.74

SIGMA AD =   8648.69

	1	2	3	4	5	6	7	8	9	10	11
2	-.87										
3	-.25	1.56									
4	-.35	-.76	0.62								
5	-.96	0.07	-.89	1.65							
6	-.95	-.20	-.89	2.78	0.73						
7	-.25	0.71	-.65	1.12	-.65	-.73					
8	2.28	2.28	0.13	0.27	-.69	-.72	0.39				
9	-.11	-.69	-.55	-.76	1.10	2.42	1.28	0.53			
10	0.07	-.56	-.04	0.20	-.92	-.94	-.65	0.38	1.08		
11	-.86	-.15	-.72	-.85	-.24	-.42	-.01	0.78	-.78	1.39	
12	0.38	-.72	-.46	-.96	-.97	-.87	-.75	1 46	-.95	-.15	-.76

The sequence of layout modifications made by subject C in group 3 and the computer's evaluation data for each layout.

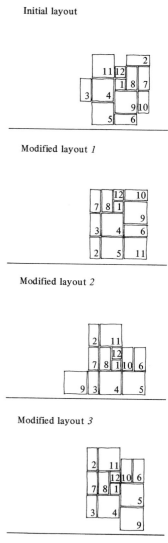

Initial layout

Modified layout *1*

Modified layout *2*

Modified layout *3*

Figure 5.13.

```
SIGMA AD =    7515.40
        1      2      3      4      5      6      7      8      9     10     11
 2   -.85
 3   -.39   1.53
 4   -.44   -.69   0.12
 5   -.97   0.14   -.85   1.16
 6   -.97   -.28   -.85   2.46   1.73
 7   -.58   -.28   -.42   2.55   -.11   -.46
 8   0.26   0.57   0.85   1.62   -.31   -.50   0.60
 9   -.44   -.71   0.25   -.37   1.42   0.62   1.44   1.01
10   -.50   -.75   1.51   0.25   -.78   -.93   -.77   0...   0.12
11   -.87   0.66   -.82   -.84   -.16   -.31   0.66   1.67   -.72   1.27
12   0.59   -.83   -.38   -.94   -.97   -.89   -.86   0.04   -.93   -.41   -.85

SIGMA AD =    7868.19
        1      2      3      4      5      6      7      8      9     10     11
 2   -.76
 3   -.52   -.06
 4   -.47   -.81   0.07
 5   -.97   -.70   -.85   1.06
 6   -.98   -.49   -.88   1.13   2.17
 7   -.60   0.74   -.78   1.33   -.21   -.42
 8   0.20   2.91   -.04   0.92   -.32   -.61   0.53
 9   -.47   -.65   0.19   -.40   2.72   0.55   2.39   1.51
10   -.65   -.62   1.02   0.05   -.71   -.90   -.61   0.09   0.07
11   -.78   0.82   -.73   -.79   -.60   -.80   1.32   3.47   -.77   1.11
12   0.52   -.55   -.44   -.94   -.96   -.92   -.86   -.01   -.95   -.74   -.56

SIGMA AD =    7974.91
        1      2      3      4      5      6      7      8      9     10     11
 2   -.81
 3   -.52   0.85
 4   -.48   -.68   0.06
 5   -.98   0.06   -.80   1.04
 6   -.98   -.41   -.85   2.26   1.58
 7   -.61   -.14   -.78   1.30   -.27   -.47
 8   0.18   1.09   -.06   0.89   -.47   -.68   0.51
 9   0.26   -.68   -.52   -.21   4.09   4.96   1.30   1.95
10   -.79   -.76   0.67   -.19   -.88   -.97   -.68   -.16   2.46
11   -.85   -.23   -.72   -.70   -.11   -.58   0.08   0.93   -.63   0.16
12   0.50   -.77   -.44   -.94   -.98   -.95   -.86   -.02   -.89   -.81   -.86

SIGMA AD =    7827.59
        1      2      3      4      5      6      7      8      9     10     11
 2   -.81
 3   -.52   0.89
 4   -.47   -.68   0.08
 5   -.98   0.08   -.79   1.07
 6   -.98   -.44   -.83   3.05   2.87
 7   -.60   -.12   -.78   1.34   -.25   -.44
 8   0.21   1.13   -.04   0.93   -.46   -.65   0.53
 9   -.02   -.54   0.20   -.40   0.04   3.18   3.31   2.65
10   -.65   -.79   1.00   0.10   -.82   -.97   -.65   -.04   1.89
11   -.85   -.22   -.71   -.70   -.10   -.64   0.10   0.96   -.59   -.15
12   0.53   -.77   -.43   -.94   -.98   -.95   -.86   -.00   -.90   -.80   -.85
```

The sequence of layout modifications made by subject D in group 3 and the computer's evaluation data for each layout.

Part 3

Anticipating the future

"But the point of cricket, surely," said Rowe, "is actually to see and appreciate the skill of the players."

"Then why are so many people content to listen to it being described on the wireless? In either case the activity of the spectator or the listener is the same—to register a selection from a range of reactions in correlation to the permutations of variables he is offered. So far as I can see, it's a finite activity, which means it's a programmable one. The spectator is eminently replaceable."

"But," said Rowe, "the spectator *enjoys* watching."

"He may, I suppose, but that's rather beside the point. The hydraulic press operator who is replaced by a computer when his factory is automated may enjoy operating a hydraulic press. But that doesn't save him from being replaced. A human being, my dear Rowe, is far too complex and expensive an instrument to be wasted on simple finite tasks like operating presses, filling up football pools, and watching cricket."

6

Simulation of computer-aided design systems

6.1 Technology assessment

Computers are a major technological innovation having a profound impact throughout society. Montagu and Snyder (1972) point out that "the computer's impact has been all the greater in that it has come so swiftly.... There are no previous examples of a technology finding such wide acceptance within so brief a period". The first successful computer was developed in 1945–1946. By 1960 there were fewer than 5000 in operation but by 1970 this number had multiplied nearly thirty times. Now, the number of computer installations worldwide is close to a quarter of a million.

Since the Industrial Revolution, technological change has seemed an inevitable fact of life in Western societies. Recently, however, a series of major criticisms of the modern technological society have come to prominence, in addition to the various energy, pollution, resources, etc crises of advanced technology. Technological 'progress' has been criticized for its ecological destruction, its deterministic tyranny, its psychological alienation, and its social disruption. We are becoming aware of the need for a comprehensive assessment of the costs and benefits of technological change.

It is in this critical and crisis-ridden atmosphere that architects are being asked to accept the most striking technological innovation in the history of their profession: the introduction of computers to the architectural design process. Understandably, most architects are variously mystified, dubious, or disturbed about the effects computers will have on the practice of design, despite the enthusiasm of the minority of their fellow architects who are in the vanguard of this particular technological progression. We have already seen, in part 2, that enthusiasm for the computer as a design aid is somewhat misplaced—at least until the machine's performance has significantly improved. But the growth of computer applications in architecture seems inexorable. Can we anticipate the effects that CAD systems will have?

As with most other major technological innovations (for example motorcars, aircraft, television), the effects of computers as experienced in various sections of society are probably a mixture of benefits and disbenefits. Because the concept of technological 'progress' has been relatively unquestioned, society has tried to cope with the disbenefits of technological change on the assumption that these are generally outweighed by the benefits. Only recently, in response to the growing criticisms and crises of modern industrial technology, has the idea of 'technology assessment' gained some limited favour.

6.1.1 Forecasting change and effect

A technology-assessment programme would attempt to forecast the effects contingent upon particular technological developments. These forecasted effects might be ranked as 'first-order', 'second-order', etc, in recognition of the way in which ripples of effects and 'side effects' are generated by technological change. Gibbon and Voyer (1973) have suggested that there is a "growing public demand for a more complete analysis of the consequences of the development of a technological capability", which, in the USA, has resulted in the establishment of an Office of Technology Assessment "as an aid to Congress, identifying possible impacts of new technological programmes".

In Britain and in the field of computer-aided architectural design, a related concept, but with a different emphasis, was included in a report of the Department of the Environment (1969). This was the suggested need for a 'look-out' institution, which would be responsible for forecasting the problems raised by introducing computers to architectural design practice. In this case, however, the 'look-out' research was intended more to find means of smoothing the way for technological change (that is, CAD), rather than to assess and perhaps question the implications of that change. Thus, a major aim of this 'look-out' research was expressed as: "To identify... obstacles to progress that could prove to be critical to the development of computer aids to building design." Obviously the crises and criticisms of modern technology that developed in the early 1970s have cast technological change in a new light. Developments such as computer applications are no longer regarded as the inevitable march of progress, from the path of which all obstacles must be removed and to which people must learn to adapt.

Perhaps fortunately for architects, their profession may well be one of the last sectors of society to undergo 'computerization'. Computer-aided design systems for architecture are still in their infancy. This could mean that architects will be fortunate enough to avoid some of the major disbenefits of computerization that may be experienced in other trades and professions that succumb earlier. In most cases, however, the full range of effects of computerization are never reported, and it therefore seems unlikely that a 'wait-and-see' attitude will on its own prove adequate as an assessment technique; other techniques are also required.

6.1.2 Systemic testing

One of the major difficulties that prevents any comprehensive assessment of the effects of technological change is simply the problem of forecasting just what the actual effects and side effects are going to be. Not until the likely effects are known can they be assessed for their desirability or undesirability. This difficulty is particularly acute where a technological change is coupled to a required behavioural change in that relatively unpredictable organism, the human being. As Jones (1967) puts it: "The

reactions of users to the existence of radically new facilities cannot be
assessed until behaviour had adapted to suit the new conditions. The
behavioural reactions of so complex an organism as the human being
in a social context cannot be foreseen without large scale tests." Jones
therefore proposed that there was a need for "test cities" that would
incorporate "simulations of new systems that are at the stage of pre-design
evaluation" for the volunteer inhabitants to test in real-life situations.

Computer-aided design systems presumably would fall into the category,
'radically new facilities' requiring such tests. The man – machine system
of designer plus computer is a new system, of which there is only
fragmentary experience to date. Simulations of computer-aided design
systems, as have in fact been carried out by the author and colleagues
(Cross, 1967; Cross et al, 1970; Evans, 1969), could provide a basic
forecasting and assessment technique.

There are two main problems which make investigation of the effects
of new computer-aided design systems difficult. First, there is the
probability that computer aids will so alter normal design processes that
speculation based entirely on conventional practice cannot be reliable.
Second, there is the prohibitive cost of setting up working experimental
systems to provide the necessary experience and feedback.

In attempting to investigate and predict the behaviour of a CAD system,
it would be misleading to extrapolate from the previous behaviour of the
system's components in isolation from one another. The most important
factor in a working system is the effect of the whole upon its parts. The
behaviour of the components is affected by their being combined into a
system—this being, of course, the very purpose of combining them. It is
these systemic behavioural patterns that need to be forecasted and assessed.

The problem is, therefore, to devise a suitable simulation of a computer-
aided design system. Current prototype systems consist essentially of a
teleprinter console, usually plus a graphic device, through which the
designer 'converses' with the computer—which may actually be some
miles from the console. All that the user perceives of the system is this
remote-access console, and the remainder is a black box to him.

Viewing the computer-aided design system in this way leads to an obvious
suggestion for a simulation technique—one may as well fill the black box
with people as with machinery. Doing so provides a comparatively cheap
simulator, with the remarkable advantages of the human operator's
flexibility, memory, and intelligence, and which can be reprogrammed to
give a wide range of computer roles merely by changing the rules of
operation. It sometimes lacks the real computer's speed and accuracy, but
a team of experts working simultaneously can compensate to a sufficient
degree to provide an acceptable simulation. This was the basic hypothesis
of the research described here.

6.2 Simulation studies

The first simulation project (Cross, 1967) established the basic methodology for the technique. The form of this project was to carry out experiments in simulating computer-aided design systems, and to observe and record the interactions, that is, the messages sent between user and 'machine', and any other relevant factors or occurrences. Much of the effort went into establishing the technique of simulation, in the hope that others might build on the experience gained, but it was also possible to generate some tentative information on the probable behaviour of real computer-aided design systems.

The basic technique used in the simulation experiments was to provide a designer (who had a prearranged problem to work on) with a means of communicating with a human 'expert computer'. Either speech or writing was the medium for communication between designer and 'computer'.

Verbal communication was used in the earlier, pilot experiments, but the majority of the twenty-three experiments were conducted with the use of written messages transmitted by a closed-circuit television link. The hardware used for communications never reached a very sophisticated level, primarily because the project was concerned with software factors, and increasing sophistication of communication hardware did not appear to alter the patterns of man–machine interaction significantly.

The project was primarily orientated towards computer-aided design of buildings, and the designers used as subjects in the experiments were generally architects. They were given the requirements for a small building to work on as a design problem during the experiments. The 'computer' was simulated by small interprofessional teams of building specialists.

No restrictions were placed on the content of the messages sent from designer to 'computer', in order that some assessment could be made of the pattern of interaction and the facilities called for in an idealized free system. There were no language restrictions imposed either, as this would have meant an undesirable learning time for the subjects and because uninhibited interaction patterns were considered to be probably the most valuable in these exploratory experiments.

How, then, did the designers respond to these idealized opportunities for using a computer-aided design system? Perhaps most important was the fact that they all found the experiments, which lasted about one hour each, very stressful and very hard work.

This feeling of stress experienced by the designers may have been largely induced by the experimental situation itself, in that the designers were aware of being 'watched'. However, the feeling of stress in working with computer-aided design systems has been confirmed by research workers in the field, with comments such as: "You get the feeling that there is nothing you can do to beat the machine". This is a point which should be worthy of careful attention, as such stress obviously could have adverse effects on the designer's capabilities, as well as limiting the duration of work periods.

6.2.1 An information retrieval system

A second project (Cross et al, 1970) used the simulation technique to investigate some of the possibilities for a computerized system to aid the designer in choosing the correct component in a design assembly. The simulation technique was used as a tool for exploring some of the questions arising from a postulated major computerized information-retrieval system for the construction industry. In particular this project was orientated towards the use of such a system for component selection during project design. Floor finish was the component selected for the project. The information now available on floor finish is in a particularly poor state, and this component often fails in use because the designer selects inappropriately from the many hundreds available.

The questions which were explored in this fairly modest study were:
1. Using 'conversational' retrieval systems, can a person who is not trained in the design discipline in which the component selection takes place, select an appropriate component? (For these purposes, such a person is called a 'naive designer'.)
2. Is it feasible to devise a question-asking procedure for the computer, which leads to the selection of an appropriate component?
3. If so, do significant differences arise between systems in which (a) the designer asks all the questions, and (b) the computer asks all the questions?

To investigate the above questions, three designers were asked to perform two experiments each, in which they would select a floor finish suitable for some design situation of their own choosing, the requirements of which they were familiar with. To aid them in their selection they had a simulated computer with which they could communicate by written messages. The 'computer' was actually two people with specialist knowledge in this field who were backed up with a store of data on floor finishes. In the first experiments, each designer asked the 'computer' whatever questions he wished, but in the second experiments the 'computer' asked all the questions.

The three designers were chosen to satisfy three types required for the study, thus:
(1)   'naive' designer with no training in building design or construction;
(2)   recently qualified, but inexperienced, architect;
(3)   qualified and experienced architect.

For analysis of results, the floor-finish attributes were divided into two groups: structural compatibility and performance requirements. This division was suggested because compatibility with the building structure is essential if a floor finish is to avoid early and serious failure, whereas to meet all of the performance requirements is not usually so essential— failure being, perhaps, only accelerated wear.

There was a significant difference between the results obtained from the 'naive' designer and those from the other two designers, in that he failed to investigate any of the structural compatibility attributes.

This suggests that 'naive' designers could probably not satisfactorily use an information retrieval system which relied entirely on the question-asking initiative coming from the designer.

The other interesting difference between the 'naive' designer and the other two was in the time taken and the number of questions asked. The qualified designers spent much longer exploring components' properties and specifying their design situation.

Further experiments suggested that 'naive' designers could use a sophisticated system such as was simulated, provided that the computer asks the designer some 'fail-safe' questions. The system could in fact be devised as a teaching aid to provide technical information where required.

In the second set of experiments the 'computer' had a prepared series of questions which it presented to the designer. These questions covered both the structural compatibility attributes (requiring yes/no answers from the designer) and the performance requirements (requiring graded answers from the designer, on a five-point scale of 0–4 for each requirement). Thus the 'computer' built for itself a design model, or profile, of site conditions and performance requirements, which it matched against the profiles of all available floor finishes. The 'computer' then output to the designer the one(s) which satisfied the design model, together with information on costs, maintenance, suppliers, etc.

There were no significant differences between the types of designer in these latter experiments, as all of them were able to answer the 'computer's' questions (although the 'naive' designer had some difficulty with building industry terminology, such as 'damp-proof membrane').

6.2.2 An intelligent system

A further project (Evans, 1969) was concerned with looking ahead to the time when computers can be expected to exhibit reasonable degrees of intelligence. The advent of machine intelligence would lead to the development of intelligent computer-aided design systems. In this situation the designer could perhaps succeed with less professional expertise than is required at present, and hence the whole design process could be accessible to designers who have little or no professional training.

In order to investigate this possibility, an intelligent computer-aided design system was simulated, and the computer functions that evolved between designer and 'computer' were analyzed. The future designer was postulated as being a 'generalist', that is less specialized and less expert than present designers. ('Naive' designers were used as an approximation to the generalist.) The 'computer' was allowed to exercise its intelligence in monitoring the designer's progress and in its responses to messages from the designer.

Ten experiments, in which communication between designer and 'computer' was a mixture of verbal and written messages and drawings, were performed. In the first three experiments, the designer and 'computer' (problem expert) merely faced each other across a table, but in the remaining experiments closed-circuit television and intercom units were used. The use of verbal messages and the inexperience of the designers could not result in the sort of explicit, structured communication of the earlier projects reported here. It was thought, however, that the resulting increased speed of message flow would reduce the likelihood that delays would interrupt the designers' working.

The designers were given one of two problems: the design of an integrated services duct, or the design of a small exhibition building. These problems had several points of dissimilarity which seemed likely to produce a variety of demands on the design system. The duct design required a lot of information to be gathered quickly, with the designer soon reaching the stage of detailed hardware design. The exhibition building design was much more complex. Both problems were intentionally fairly small, so that a range of design techniques would be required in the one to two hours spent on them.

In general it was found from the experiments that the resulting design work produced solutions which were useable but not very efficient. The simulated computer system was not entirely adequate to support a designer of so little experience as the 'naive' designer, but it seems likely that a 'generalist' designer (much less specialized than present designers) could be adequately supported by such a system.

A more detailed review of the above projects has been provided by the author elsewhere (Cross, 1972c).

The effects of computer aids

7.1 Effects on the individual designer

What will be the ripples of effects and side effects as CAD systems are introduced to architectural design practice? There is a pressing need for some prediction of the impact of the computer on architectural design (Cross, 1972a). This chapter tries to develop some predictions of the effects of CAD, both on the individual designer and on the design process.

The forecasts and assessments of effects that are presented here have been derived from three principal sources. First, from the simulation studies carried out by the author and colleagues, as reviewed in the previous chapter. Second, from relevant reports on the effects of computerization in fields other than architectural design. Third, from what little is already known of the effects of prototype systems and part systems for computer-aided architectural design.

7.1.1 Stress

The most important finding relevant to the present context that emerged from the first simulation study (Cross, 1967) was that all the designers who used the simulated CAD system found it very stressful. This stress was in part due to the nature of the experimental situation itself, but was also obviously due to the speed and accuracy with which the designer was now seemingly inevitably expected to work. This feeling of stress is commonly reported by those who have used prototype on-line CAD systems.

In both the first and the second simulation study (Cross et al, 1970) it seemed that factors contributing to this stress were: the designer knows that the computer has large files of information stored away, but, being a machine, it tends to behave 'stupidly' instead of 'helpfully'; because the designer knows that accurate information *is* available, he feels it incumbent upon himself to attempt to retrieve the most relevant piece of this information; using the computer leaves an often permanent, and public, record of the designer's sequence of actions, which should therefore be able to stand up to scrutiny by colleagues; computers are known to be expensive, and therefore their time should not be 'wasted'.

To some extent such findings may be dependent on the type of task that is being computerized, and the way in which the computer application is itself designed. Mumford and Banks (1967) conducted case studies of the introduction of computerized procedures in two firms (a bank and a foodstuffs company). They found that, with some of the computerized procedures, the number of variables to be considered by the decisionmaker would be significantly reduced by the computer, thus removing some of the 'challenge' of the job. They also noted, however, that with traditional procedures "relatively incompetent executives were able to hide their limitations because they rationalised that 'no-one could possibly have enough of the relevant facts to make a decision'. With the use of a computer, the number of facts that they could consider was greatly increased and so was their anxiety about making decisions. Bad decision-taking would be less easily excused by senior management because crucial variables could be identified by the computer".

The parallels with aspects of decisionmaking in architectural practice seem very clear. Architects might therefore expect a similar increase in anxiety resulting from the use of computers in their work.

7.1.2 Intensification of work rate

Cooley (1972) also suggests that stress will be induced in the users of CAD systems, principally by the intensification of work rate to which computers tend to lead. Cooley refers to a study by the Department of Labor in the United States, which "assessed that a designer doing a job in the aerospace industry spent 95% of his time undertaking reference work and only 5% on actual design decision-making. The introduction of computer graphic systems can eliminate the routine reference work and actually intensify the decision-making rate by up to 1900%. The stress this will put upon the design staff involved can be enormous".

The fact that conventional, drawing-board design work is almost wholly self-paced is emphasized by Cooley, who fears that the introduction of computers will mean that designers will be paced by the machine. "In the past, the freedom to walk about to a library to gain reference material was almost a therapeutic necessity. The opportunities to discuss design problems with one's colleagues often resulted in a useful cross-fertilisation of ideas, and in a resultant better design. As more and more interactive systems are evolved and software packages built up for them, man's knowledge will be absorbed from him at an ever increasing rate, and stored in the system."

There is some confirmation of this in the study of a simulated computer-aided information retrieval system for building design (Cross et al, 1970) This study compared two types of system; one in which the computer played a passive, library-like role, and one in which there was a more active role for the computer, based on a predetermined interrogatory sequence that the computer put to the designer. In this latter role the computer had 'absorbed' the knowledge of how to proceed rationally, and imposed this procedure on the designer. This was found to be much more efficient: "The time taken to reach an acceptable solution was greatly reduced... being only 10 to 15 minutes. This must compare very favourably with the time taken to reach an equally certain decision in (conventional) practice".

7.1.3 Reduction of staff

As a trade-union leader, Cooley is concerned not only with the stress induced by working with computers, but also with the implications of the change from labour-intensive work patterns in the conventional design office towards capital-intensive patterns as the expensive computers are introduced. He suggests that some companies are "concentrating their design power in specialised computer centres, whilst at the same time they are declaring staff redundant elsewhere. The staff engaged at the design centres are being compelled to work either consistent overtime or on shift, whilst their colleagues have to join the dole queue".

Most design professionals, such as architects, will doubtless consider themselves to be somewhat more immune to the consequences of computerization that Cooley predicts for the design draughtsman. However, economic savings will have to be made somewhere if the expense of a computer installation is to be met. This inevitably means somehow saving man-hours, either by a reduced time scale for the overall design process (with consequent stress) or by a reduction in required design man hours. Since the total amount of work available to architects is unlikely to grow much, however, savings in the design process cannot be translated into taking on more work for the same manpower as currently exists. The result therefore would seem to be a reduction in the number of design staff required.

Reduction in 'staff costs' was apparently the only quantifiable 'benefit' that could be found in a cost–benefit analysis of implementing the CEDAR system in the Department of the Environment design offices (Chalmers, 1972). Chalmers suggests that lower staff costs would be achieved by increases in 'design productivity'. The increase in productivity necessary to justify the capital investment in, and running costs of such a CAD system, was found to be one and a half to two times—that is, halving the design manpower.

Auger (1972) states it as a "fact" (derived presumably from his own experience in developing a commercially viable, comprehensive CAD system for architects) that "the application of office computer systems must greatly reduce the need for architectural assistance in the drawing office". The restructuring of office procedures that is implicit in the adoption of computer systems will determine where the axe will fall. This restructuring will be discussed later.

7.1.4 New tasks

It also seems inevitable that an immediate effect of the use of computers is the introduction of new technical tasks such as data preparation, program writing and debugging, tape or card punching, etc. These 'machine-minding' tasks that accompany computer-aided design are generally of a kind that most designers are psychologically averse to, since the tasks are low-level, tedious, and time-consuming, whilst demanding high levels of concentration. A task such as the digital coding of information from drawings, for example, seems hardly likely to be a popular new task in the design office, even given sophisticated machine aids.

7.1.5 Threats and promises

Against these potential 'threats' of stress, anxiety, increased pace of work, redundancy, and machine-minding tasks, it should perhaps be said that there are also potential 'promises' arising from the use of computer systems. An optimistic projection of the computer-aided architect is as the efficient operator of an automated drawing board which incorporates graphic displays and various input–output devices coupled to sophisticated computer programs. Thus aided, the architect would be able to optimize solutions to the rational aspects of design, whilst being liberated from mundane activities so as to be able creatively to pursue the intuitive aspects.

Cooley (1973) regards this as a rather naive view which ignores "the real economic and political context in which CAD is being introduced to the design environment". He suggests that "it would be both foolish and elitist to believe that the work in which we as designers are engaged is so complex that the consequences will not be similar to that which has been experienced on the shop floor". This experience suggests that, within a capitalist system, capital (equipment) receives first consideration, people come second. Cooley warns that "this subordination of the operator to the machine is now spreading right through the design spectrum. There are those involved in highly creative fields, such as architects, who seem to believe that these problems would never extend into their preserves. In fact systems now exist such as the Harness system, where the architect is reduced to disposing predetermined architectural elements about a 'harness'. Clearly his creative scope is thereby limited."

The impending changes to the architect's job may also be seen by optimists as part of a wider pattern of changes in employment. Despite the short-term problems of automation, the emerging role of the computer in society could be to relieve human beings of the need to maintain hour-by-hour and day-by-day control of production functions. In that case, the current work/leisure, job/home, etc distinctions would disappear, leaving minimal work responsibilities which could be conducted with the aid of a home computer terminal and a public-utility information system (see for example Sackman, 1967).

However, Cooley (1972) remains adamant that the "harsh reality" of the introduction of high-capital equipment, such as CAD equipment, "is very different from that envisaged by some Utopian Socialists who used to write books about the problems of people spending their leisure time when the work was automated and computerised. It is also in glaring contrast with those predictions that high capital equipment in the technological areas would simply liberate people from routine tasks and free them to devote themselves more fully to creative activities."

7.2 Effects on the design process

According to Esher and Llewellyn-Davies (1968), we have been experiencing "a fundamental series of changes in the practice of architecture, which began seriously in the 1940's and will not be complete for at least 20 more years". It is therefore sometimes difficult to isolate changes in the architectural design process which are solely attributable to the effects of introducing computer systems. The architectural design process is already changing under the pressure of other forces. These related pressures for change have been identified in a report by the Department of the Environment (1969).

Three main areas of foreseeable changes in the building industry were identified:

1. building management—changes from the traditional pattern of operations towards those offered by package-deal builders and industrialized building system manufacturers;

2. building construction—improvement of on-site working conditions, and continued evolution from labour-intensive to capital-intensive production methods;

3. built forms—trends towards the incorporation of greater adaptibility, or flexibility, in both the exterior and interior building elements.

An overall change in the structure of the total design–build–use process which was forecast in the Department of the Environment report was the inversion of the present pattern of effort applied over the process (figure 7.1). Currently the process is organized with a large 'hump' of effort in the middle, around the generation of production information— working drawings, schedules, etc (figure 7.2). The general changes referred to above, such as the use of industrialized building systems, are already operating to depress this 'hump' and to shift some of the design effort towards either end of the total process.

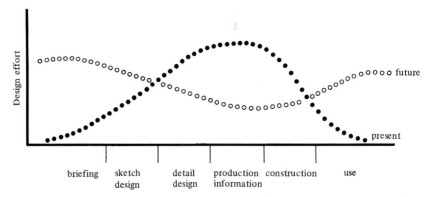

Figure 7.1. The expected inversion of the pattern of design effort over the total brief-design–build–use process.

For example, in the earliest stages of the overall process, that is, briefing and sketch design, there are trends towards research and development groups working in client organizations, and towards the modelling of space-activity interactions so as to allow activity scheduling and space division to proceed in parallel. The use of industrialized building systems drastically reduces the need to prepare detailed construction drawings for each job, and simplifies the preparation of schedules of components, at the production-information stage. They also tend to reduce on-site monitoring, etc during the construction stage. However, the advent of adaptable buildings to meet changing user requirements has introduced the concept of 'design-in-use', which requires continued design effort during the use stage.

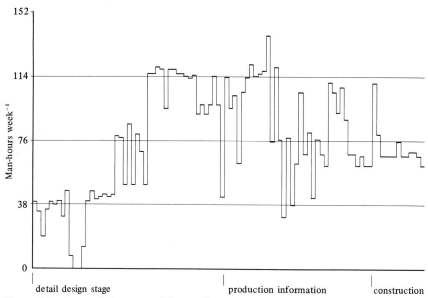

Figure 7.2. A recorded pattern of design effort over part of a typical project. (From a study of the building timetable by the Building Economics Research Unit, 1968).

7.2.1 Briefing

Computer-aided design systems will amplify these changes. The briefing, sketch-design, and design-in-use stages, for example, can take advantage of new computer models for the design and allocation of spaces and/or activities. Maver (1972) has described computer programs that help provide "a systematic approach to the problem of flexibility in educational buildings", for instance. These programs enable a much closer 'fit' to be achieved between the schedule of accommodation and the actual activity pattern to be accommodated, resulting in significant space savings.

E

Some of the implications that such computer aids for the briefing stage would have for architects, clients, and building users have been demonstrated by Davies (1975). As part of a research programme within a local-authority Architect's Department, Davies applied a space/timetable allocation program to test a proposal for an extension to an existing secondary school to accommodate a new intake of sixty sixth-form pupils. The program used was part of the SPACES suite of programs for accommodation scheduling, layout generation, and appraisal of schools (described in chapter 3). The results of the computer application suggested that the existing space in the school could be used more efficiently and that there was no need for the proposed extension. These results were adopted by the Director of Education of the local authority concerned, and a feasibility study for the extension which had been undertaken by a private architectural practice was taken no further.

This research by Davies exposed an anomaly in the relationship between architect and client. It was the Architect's Department that discovered there was no need for the new building, but the 'need' decisions are in fact the prerogative of, in this instance, the Director of Education's Department. Davies commented, "Fortunately, the Director appreciated the conclusion reached, but in future exercises his staff should be involved at the earliest stages. The Advisory Staff who are responsible to the Director of Education for the preparation of Briefs for school buildings, quite understandably have expressed concern over the need to apply such a tool as SPACES together with the experience and training of specialist officers."

No doubt it was not only the client's advisory staff who were perturbed; the private architects who were involved might also be excused a little chagrin at losing a potential commission. One might also expect the teachers involved to regret the loss of potential extra teaching space, but Davies reports that they were in fact most cooperative, which was fortunate since the necessary collection of data on timetables, etc required their extensive cooperation. This vital cooperation might not of course always be so readily available once the typical results of the SPACES computer exercise become known.

Indeed, a very similar exercise in another county met quite a different response, according to a report by Derbyshire (1975), who was a research-student observer of the exercise. This exercise was to determine an optimal schedule of accommodation for a new school building, but it met severe problems of communication between the CAD experts, the teachers, the administrators, and the architect. There was also some distrust by the teachers of the whole aim of the exercise. Derbyshire reports that "some of the educationalists doubted the relevance of an 'optimal' schedule, since it ignored the problems of moving equipment, pupils and teachers". There was a feeling on the part of the teachers that the resulting schedule would be far too rigid. They were therefore reluctant to produce the necessary data "for fear that the computer would produce 'the answer'".

The exercise was not successful, and the architect and administrators eventually resorted to determining the schedule by conventional means.

However, these types of computer applications do have the merit of involving the users of buildings in some of the design decisionmaking from which they are conventionally excluded. The connection between computer aids and user participation in design has been developed by Cross and Maver (1973): "Users' involvements with their buildings have been in two main areas—either early in the design process, during the briefing and preliminary design stages, or very late on, actually modifying the building in use. Both of these areas need some aids if they are to progress beyond their current limitations. Principally, they need a common language for user and designer to share during the early stages, and a similar (perhaps the same) common language for user and designer to share during the continuous reconstruction of flexible buildings. The common language(s) could be already emerging in the predictive models of the computer programs."

7.2.2 Production information

Computerization of the production-information procedures, such as computer selection and combination of standard details, computer-produced schedules and drawings, and computer-aided information retrieval, should drastically reduce the amount of effort needed at that stage of the process. In an evaluation study, it was found by Thompson and Hughes (1974) that the prototype CEDAR computer-aided design system reduced the elapsed time for the design of the structural frame of a building ("from the initiation of frame design to loaded, coded, scheduled and final drawn layouts") from the typical forty-eight days of the current manual process to just two days. Thompson and Hughes further estimated that the CEDAR system when fully operational would reduce this elapsed time to only one day.

New patterns of organization of the design process must inevitably arise from such drastic changes. It could be the introduction of design shift-work, as Cooley (1972; 1973) warns, or it could be that short bursts (one–two hours) of the highly intensive CAD work will be separated by longer periods of relaxation. This latter suggestion is in line with the optimistic view of the role of machines and automation procedures as liberators, rather than enslavers, of mankind (for example Thring, 1973).

7.2.3 The management pyramid

Within the office new structures of responsibility and control would accompany the introduction of CAD systems. "The introduction of computer systems into architects' offices", Auger (1972) suggests, "would clearly bring about major changes in the method of working and in the composition of the typical office. The designer in charge of a project would be able to assemble personally the major sections and, except in the case of a very large project, he would also be able to prepare the final drawings and schedules unaided apart from the computer."

Mumford and Banks (1967), on the basis of their studies of the
introduction of computerized office procedures, stress that technical
change of this kind inevitably changes human roles and relationships within
the office. They report that one principal effect of computerization is a
flattening of the pyramid of management hierarchy (figure 7.3). This
is because the handling of data by the computer can lead to a reduced
need for middle management, by making wider spans of control possible
for senior management. Similarly Auger (1972) suggests that, in a large
architect's office, computer systems would eliminate "the four or five
echelons of staff down which information is passed". If for economic
reasons the introduction of computer systems means a reduction in
manpower, then these reductions will be made in the middle-management
'echelons'.

The hierarchical structure of the modern architectural practice, as
outlined by Auger, is comprised of "as many as three levels of partners
and associates, with senior assistants, assistants and technicians plus, of
course, librarians, secretaries, typists and print boys". The effect of
computerization on this pyramid should be, therefore, to reduce the need

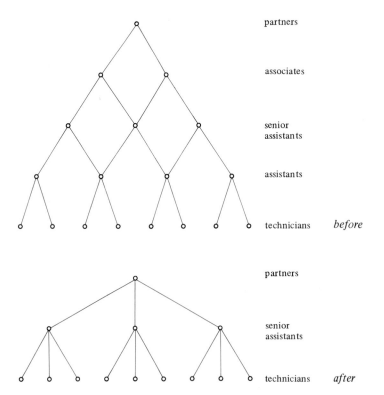

Figure 7.3. The effect of computerization on the management pyramid.

for some levels of associate partners and the intermediate level of assistant architects. The technicians, we know, are likely to maintain their job security, although they perhaps will be involved in the new kinds of machine-minding tasks; the senior assistants will bear the brunt of the stressful on-line CAD work; and the partners in the practice will be relieved of any pressure from below from their associates.

7.2.4 The change agents

One other finding of Mumford and Banks also seems relevant in this context. This is related to the fact that computers bring with them a group of people who are very different from the usual office worker. This new group of 'change agents'—the programmers, consultants, systems analysts, and so on—have personal and collective goals that are quite separate from those of the organizations within which they (temporarily) work.

It is perhaps instructive to read the comments of Mumford and Banks on these change agents as they appeared in banking offices, whilst bearing the parallel of architectural offices in mind: "A group with an entirely new approach to work had therefore appeared in the bank environment. Their work interest depended on change, they had no contact with customers and little with branch activity; in addition they had considerable market value and might easily be tempted to leave the bank for better-paid jobs in outside industry. The bank, for the first time, was presented with a junior management group who were no longer completely identified with banking." In computer-aided architectural design the change agents, significantly, already tend to be a group of people "no longer completely identified" with architecture. They establish and reinforce their peer group images at conferences and meetings where architecture, as such, is rarely—if ever—discussed.

7.2.5 Roles and relationships in the building team

Of course it is not only the architect whose job will be fundamentally affected by CAD systems. Roles and relationships between the different specialists involved in the total building-design process also seem likely to be affected. At the moment the architect tends to play a central role in coordinating the activities and design inputs of the other specialists. The proposers of comprehensive computer systems for the building industry (for example Building Research Station, 1969), however, foresee continuous, rather than the current intermittent, collaboration between specialists, with the computer being the medium through which this collaboration is effected (figure 7.4). Note that the computer occupies the central role that architects have traditionally presumed to be their own role as the 'leaders of the building team'.

In such a comprehensive system all the participants in the design process would use common data files and a common representation within the computer of the current state of the design proposals. Integration and coordination of the specialist contributions to the project would be made by the computer, with each specialist able to have immediate evaluation of the implications of modifications to his own contribution. One side effect of systems such as this would be to remove the present scope for shielding one's own inadequacies from the rest of the team by using specialist jargon and hypothetical specialist difficulties. Similar effects on decisionmakers were found by Mumford and Banks, as referred to earlier.

Even without the introduction of large-scale comprehensive computer systems in the building industry, new relationships and patterns of communication between participants in the design process could accompany the growing use of commercial time-sharing computer systems. For example, where an architect and, say, a quantity surveyor are engaged on the same project, and both use the same time-sharing system, it seems obvious that they will set up common computer files for the project. There are already some indications of this happening, as reported (Cross and Maver, 1970) in a survey of user experience with time-sharing terminals.

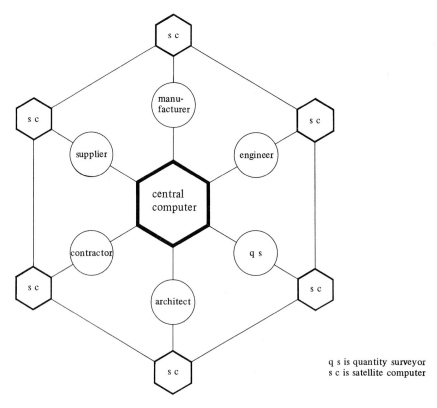

q s is quantity surveyor
s c is satellite computer

Figure 7.4. Representation of a typical model of an information system for the building industry, based on a central computer. Besides having access to the national central computer, the participants in each project are often assumed to share common files accessed through and linked by individual satellite computers.

The current professional barriers which tend to restrict the potential for interprofessional collaboration could limit further developments of this kind.

One other effect of a common computerized information system for the building industry could be to open up communication links which hardly exist at all at the moment. Manufacturers of building components, for instance, could use a central building-industry computer to gather data on trends in component selection in order to keep abreast of these trends and to modify their component ranges accordingly.

7.2.6 User participation

By making the design process more open and explicit, computers also open the way for a wider range of participants to contribute to the process. In particular the users of buildings, who have traditionally been allowed no participation in the design process, could become involved in a computer-aided process.

Mitchell (1972) for example has argued that, potentially, some computer systems "will result in an opening-up of architectural and urban design processes to wider and truer participation by making it possible for non-specialists to comprehend and directly manipulate quite powerful models of the environment".

Speaking of the City-Scape type of dynamic visual simulation, Woodruff (1969) hypothesized the following scenario. "Picture, if you will, a Sunday evening TV programme in colour.... They are playing a tape which shows the latest (local) urban renewal plans. First you would see a simulated overall view of the development, perhaps even an aerial perspective. The picture would then shift to the viewpoint of someone driving through the development, later getting out of the car and walking in between some of the buildings. Following a complete tour of the exterior of the project, the TV simulation would move through a door for a preview of the interior of the building. As long as the interior could be described by the architect, each room or type of room could be simulated by the computer and shown to the TV audience. All this is done before a single nail is driven."

A formal mechanism for this participation in design has been proposed by Maver (1970), who suggests that a 'solution team' composed of clients, users, and others affected by a building proposal should be involved in an iterative process of appraising design proposals. Initial proposals from the design team would be subject to computer appraisals, then the alternative proposals and appraisals would be submitted to the solution team who would vote on the alternatives. The voting patterns would then be fed back to the design team as information on which to base modifications of the design proposals. Thus a suggestion for restructuring the design process has stemmed from considering the implications of computer-aided design systems.

Interestingly Cakin (1976) has shown that, given 'sophisticated' information on alternative design proposals—that is cost and performance information such as might be available from a computer evaluation program—groups of nonarchitects reach the same conclusion as groups of architects do on their preferences for alternative proposals. A 'solution team's' judgements would therefore appear to be as 'sophisticated' as the information with which it is presented. (Incidentally, without the 'sophisticated' information, groups of architects disagree much more amongst themselves than nonarchitects do.)

More radical proposals suggest that the 'middle man'—the architect—in this iterative design-and-test process could be dispensed with, and the users allowed to develop their own building designs by direct interaction with the computer. The Architecture Machine Group (1971) for example have said, "We propose to take a step towards allowing the urban dweller to participate in the design of his own environment by multiplying the availability of design services... We propose to multiply both the number of designers (machines), and the number of people to whom design services can be made available." This may be seen as a logical implication of their work towards a robot architect.

A question that remains to be resolved is how much designing would actually be done by the client/user and how much by the machine. Simply to exchange the human architect for a machine architect would not necessarily increase the user's 'participation' in design.

Coleman (1973) has developed a prototype CAD system which ostensibly could increase user participation in housing design. This system enables the user to arrange on the computer's display screen a number of graphic symbols within a given boundary. The symbols are conventional graphic representations of rooms in a house—bedrooms, kitchen, bathroom, etc. The boundary is assumed to be the limit of space available—it could represent the boundary walls of one flat in a block, or the exterior wall boundary of a standard house pattern. Within this boundary the potential occupant(s) could arrange the rooms to suit personal requirements or desires. The role of the computer is to prevent 'illegal' arrangements (for example, violations of building regulations) and to provide evaluations of the user's proposals. Coleman suggests that "this study has gone some way towards providing a system that can guide a non-expert designer towards developing realistic and lively layouts of his future home and towards establishing a computing system which can ultimately result in a return to a more socially evolved architecture, an architecture relating more closely to life."

Evans (1969), in the simulation studies reviewed earlier, has already pursued the idea that the advent of more 'intelligent' computer-aided design systems would mean that the designer could succeed with less professional expertise than is required at present. Hence the whole design process could be accessible to designers who have little or no professional training. He found that the design solutions produced during the course of the experiments, by nonprofessional designers, were generally of poor quality. The simulated 'intelligent' computer system was not, therefore, entirely adequate to support a 'naive' designer. A 'generalist' designer, though, Evans suggested, could be adequately supported by such a system. A lessening of the highly skilled specialism of current design training could thus become a realistic proposition with intelligent computer-aided design systems.

As building technology (adaptable buildings) and computer applications (intelligent machines) evolve towards each other, Negroponte (1972) amongst others, has suggested a further possibility—the development of a 'responsive' architecture in which an adaptable environment is enhanced with machine intelligence. Thus a building might get to 'know' its occupants; it would change its facilities to meet their requirements, and adapt its behaviour to suit theirs. Living in a building and designing that building would therefore become one process, and 'design' as a separate process, activity, or job would cease to exist.

In order to summarize the possible effects of computers in design, discussed in this chapter, the contrasting threats and promises of computer-aided design are given in table 7.1

Table 7.1. Scenarios for the future: the contrasting threats and promises of computer-aided architectural design. The 'promises' have been more widely publicized as the probable future of CAAD, but the 'threats' seem an equally probable reality.

Promises	Threats
The architect is portrayed as skilfully operating a battery of sophisticated design aids ranging from a semiautomatic drawing board to large-screen CRT displays of 'walk around' views of the proposed building.	The architect is seen surrounded by a buzzing, flashing, chattering confusion of computer hindrances poorly designed to match his limited human abilities in handling quantitative data.
The architectural design process is significantly increased in efficiency, both in terms of the time taken to design and detail a new project, and in terms of the handling of a greatly increased quantity and range of data affecting the project.	Speeding-up the design process leads to greater pressure of work on the architect, and working on-line with computers is very stressful. Handling more data in a more 'open' way creates anxiety for the architect.
The boring 'grunge' work of detailing, scheduling, drawing, etc is taken over by the machine, leaving the architect more time and freedom to pursue the creative aspects of design.	Considerable time, money, and effort are spent in 'machine minding'—punching cards or tapes, writing programs, tracing errors, maintaining the machinery and waiting for it to be repaired after breakdowns.
The architect's role as the 'leader' of the building design 'team' is reinforced by his enhanced powers of information handling via the computer system.	The computer becomes the key 'member' at the centre of the building 'team', with the architect playing a reduced role on the periphery.

continued overleaf

E*

Table 7.1. (continued)

Promises	*Threats*
The architect approaches more nearly his ideal of the Renaissance 'Universal Man', handling, with computer help, a variety of design projects with consummate creativity.	The architect is dominated by the 'change agents' who create the computer programs and systems, rigidly constraining the projects the architect may take on and the types of solution he may propose.
Smaller, more effective, more 'democratic' working groups can be formed in the architect's office for each design project, using the computer to integrate the work of the office and the groups, and to take on much of the work on individual projects.	A rigid, hierarchical bureaucratization is imposed on the architect's office by computer systems which demand clearly defined 'chains of command' and only a few 'decisionmakers' backed up by an army of technicians.
With the computer relieving the architect of much of his day-to-day work, considerable job flexibility will be possible, including working at home and at many other nonoffice locations, and at times to suit personal preferences.	The capital cost of the computer equipment has to be offset by a reduction in staff employed in architectural offices, with consequent redundancy and unemployment problems for architects. Those still employed have to work shifts to keep the machinery running.
The computer offers new possibilities in the way of data manipulation and the production of a variety of information other than conventional limited drawings.	The computer disrupts and destroys the architect's traditional skills in the preparation and interpretation of drawings, causing confusion and costly errors in the interpretation of alternative modes of presentation of information.
An improved quality of building design results from the use of computer aids which allow more design factors to be taken into consideration, a higher number of potential solutions to the design problem to be considered, a more exhaustive testing of the proposed solutions, and a greater degree of refinement to be made to the preferred solution.	Quantitative data drive out qualitative: largely irrelevant numerical data swamp the design process because only such data can be handled by the computer, with a resultant loss of architectural values in building design. CAD systems are environmental-variety reducers, producing a narrow range of pseudo-optimum building designs in a small number of monotonous building systems.
Computers will 'deprofessionalize' the design process, allowing laypeople greater access to, and involvement in, the process. Laypeople will be able to design their own buildings with computer aid. Wider participation in design will democratize the building design process, avoiding the whimsical, perverse excesses of 'prima donna' professional designers.	Computer power will equal design power: those who can afford the expensive computer systems will dominate the design process. Design power will be centralized in large organizations, and the design process will become bureaucratized, with greatly reduced scope for private individuals to influence the design of their built environment.
Computers will be built into the building fabric, and these computer-controlled buildings will precisely and rapidly adapt themselves to changing environmental conditions and the requirements of their inhabitants. A responsive, 'intelligent' environment will result.	Automatic control of buildings will result in a machine dictatorship, rigidly controlling access to, and use of, buildings. Computer breakdowns and malfunctionings will send buildings haywire, with results ranging from mild chaos to loss of life.

Part 4

Design systems design

"The whole world of sport, I believe, will gradually become an entirely enclosed one, unvisited by any human being except the maintenance engineers. Computers will play. Computers will watch. Computers will comment. Computers will store results, and pit their memories against other computers in sports quiz programmes on the television organised by computers and watched by computers."

"Y-e-e-e-es," said Rowe.

Michael Frayn *The Tin Men*

8

Human and machine roles in design

8.1 The need for assessment
The last four chapters have tried to develop an anticipatory assessment of the impact that computer-aided design systems might have in architectural applications. The conclusions of this assessment can only be regarded as very tentative at this stage, given the limitations of the available knowledge. This anticipatory assessment indicates chiefly, perhaps, the areas where further research is necessary. Even so, the interim and tentative conclusions should be worrying to architects.

8.1.1 Effects and effectiveness
There are three major areas in which one may assess the *effects* that CAAD systems might have for the architect and the architectural design process. First, there are the effects on the day-to-day working life of the architect —on architectural design as a job. This job could change radically. Notably, for the individual designer, CAD systems pose threats of stress and anxiety, through intensifying his work rate and making public and assessable his decisionmaking.

Second, there are the areas of change where the computer meshes with and promotes a broad set of related changes. Computer-aided design systems will catalyze these other factors which affect the design process, and will amplify the changes that are leading to a reduction of the design effort applied in some parts of the process. This reduction of effort may well lead to problems of redundancy, particulary at 'middle-management' levels.

The third major area where we might draw some conclusions on the effect of CAD is in the structure of the design team. Roles, relationships, and patterns of communication between the architect and other participants in the design process are very likely to change under the impact of computer systems. Generally this change will be towards a more 'open' structure. In the long term, CAD systems could also make the design process accessible to a wider range of participants. In particular the explicit aim of some CAD developments is towards user participation in design—even, eventually, user control of the design process.

Regarding the assessment of the *effectiveness* of CAD systems, it seems that, for the moderately sized design problems used in the experiments reported here, there are no overwhelming differences between human and machine performances. In highly constrained problems, the machine tends to produce results approximately 6% better than those of the humans. In less constrained, more 'real world' problems, however, the machine does not perform so well and humans (given adequate but modest time to produce their solutions) tend to produce results approximately 4% better than those of the machine.

Man-machine symbiosis is also still a long way off if the results of the
experiments with an 'interactive' CAD system are typical. The man-
machine mode, as used in these experiments, tended to produce worse
results than either humans or machines alone. Man-machine results were
approximately 6% worse than those of unaided humans, and approximately
2% worse than machine results. The concept of interactive man-machine
problem solving would seem to need to be reorientated significantly from
that of the evaluative program used in these experiments.

In general we might conclude that the assessment attempted here has
indicated that computer-aided architectural design systems may have wide
effects but limited effectiveness.

That wide-ranging effects would be associated with the introduction of
computers to the design process is perhaps only to be expected. A lack
of effectiveness in terms of the overall efficiency of the design process and
the measurable criteria (quite apart from the unmeasurable ones) of the
design product is more surprising, and doubtless will be disputed by the
change agents. But until further experimental evidence is forthcoming, it
seems that architects could justifiably maintain a certain scepticism about
the performance of the machine as a designer.

8.1.2 Lack of knowledge

At the moment there is simply insufficient evaluation of either the effects
or the effectiveness of CAD systems. Willey (1976) for example, bemoans
the fact that "no studies have been carried out which clearly demonstrate
the advantages of a CAD system for architectural sketch design". After
a review of computer systems that purport to aid sketch design, he
suggests that "there does not appear to be any immediate benefit to be
gained from using the computer system except its novelty and apparent
sophistication", and "the problem remains that no computer-based design
tool to date has demonstrably increased the architect's abilities during
sketch design". Thompson and Hughes (1974) also report that their
literature search has shown that "whilst considerable effort has been
expended on the evaluation of military and commercial man-computer
systems, little direct experimental evidence concerning the performance of
design systems is available. The situation is especially unsatisfactory in
computer-aided building design, where it was found that unsupported
qualitative and quantitative statements... are the *only* performance guides...".

Trying to improve this lack-of-knowledge situation, Thompson and
Hughes (1974) made their own evaluation of a part of the CEDAR
computer-aided building design system concerned with the design of the
structural frame. They claim that designers were able to reduce structural
frame capital costs by 7% - 8% by using CEDAR in an iterative redesign
process, although no comparisons were made with what a manual redesign
process might achieve. However, they also found that "CEDAR as at present
implemented on ATLAS would be barely competitive" with conventional

manual procedures on economic grounds (limited effectiveness?), but that, for the structural frame design process, "manually the process takes approximately 48 days, compared with 2 days on prototype CEDAR" (wide effects?). Perhaps the apparently paradoxical conclusion of wide effects but limited effectiveness will not be unusual as more evaluations of this kind are made.

It is the need for much more of this experimental evidence (and of greater scientific rigour) that is worth stressing here. Too frequently the CAD system designers and developers—the change agents—leave their systems' performances unquantified and unevaluated; a take-it-or-leave-it attitude to design which they would be quick to condemn in other designers.

8.1.3 Inadequate reporting

In the meanwhile we are forced to glean what little evidence we can from passing comments buried in the generally glowing accounts of how well prototype systems are operating in practice. For example Weinzapfel and Handel (1975) include a brief 'review of applications' in their report of IMAGE, an interactive spatial-layout program.

They report that "several student projects" using IMAGE "met with surprising success", although they do not say why they should find the success of their own system surprising. Perhaps one reason for this apparent success was that the student architects using IMAGE worked "harder and for longer periods than they did in their conventional studios". Weinzapfel and Handel attribute this increase in effort to "the added entertainment value of the computer display", but offer no details of any extrinsic motivation that might also have applied, such as whether the students were constrained to use IMAGE in competition for assessment with other students working in conventional studios. It is just this lack of rigorous reporting of 'experiments' that makes the confidence that the 'experimenters' tend to have in their 'results' so unnerving.

Weinzapfel and Handel nevertheless do at least admit that "of course, not all aspects of these experiments were successful". The students tended, for one thing, to let IMAGE retain the design initiative: "Even when it was clear that IMAGE was not improving a poor arrangement, students were quite willing to have it continue trying rather than intervene with ideas of their own". And, despite the fact that they were working harder with IMAGE, "a majority of the students believed that they could have achieved satisfactory designs quicker without the aid of IMAGE." These experimenters are also sufficiently candid to admit that, although IMAGE may be advantageous in practice for large, complex design projects, for more modest projects "the benefits of using the system may not be sufficient to warrant its use".

Such candour in reporting the limitations of a CAD system is unusual. It is much more usual to attempt to squeeze the maximum apparent advantage from the results of any system assessment. In general, what one might otherwise have taken for granted is reported as a positive advantage to the machine. Thus, Shirley (1974) reports in a distinctly positive style that the machine (in this case a program for allocating positions of lifts in a Harness hospital design) was at least *no worse* than the architect: "The lift placing algorithm has always produced results which are as efficient or more efficient than the architects' lift placements".

Shirley compares human and machine performances in this instance in terms of their abilities to keep the total value of circulation movement in a given Harness hospital design to a minimum, whilst being constrained within a maximum number of lifts available. The design task is therefore the judicious placing of these lifts. Shirley suggests that the lift-placing program has been tested on twelve Harness hospital schemes, but reports the results of only one 'example'. The architect chose lift positions which gave a total circulation value $2 \cdot 9\%$ greater than an 'ideal' value which would be obtained if there were lifts everywhere—that is outside every department entrance. The machine chose slightly different lift positions which gave a total circulation value $2 \cdot 35\%$ greater than the 'ideal'. The difference between $2 \cdot 9\%$ and $2 \cdot 35\%$ Shirley has to admit "is only a small improvement". Whether this trivial result is in any way meaningful is not reported.

8.1.4 How difficult is designing?

Perhaps, after all, the quantifiable aspects of architectural design are just not as difficult as the computer systems' protagonists would suggest? We might possibly conclude this from a report by Berger et al (1974) of some experiments with a General Decision Model (GDM) computer program and its application to space-planning problems. To establish the relevance of the optimization procedure of the GDM, Berger et al first established some data on random solutions to a modest architectural design problem. They defined this as a general problem in terms of a multistoreyed rectangular building on a rectangular flat site, to be designed within a set of nine variables: site depth and breadth, building depth and breadth, internal corridor width, number of storeys, storey height, useable floor area, and percentage of glazed area on the facade. To define a particular problem, each of these variables was then given lower and upper bounds (for example, glazed area between 10% and 100%) or constrained in other appropriate ways (for example, fixing the site dimensions and controlling the relationship of glazing area to room depth). In summary the problem might be considered to represent the significant quantifiable variables in a typical outline office-building design.

Berger et al generated by computer 1000 random solutions to this problem, and costed each (in monetary terms) by means of a standard costing formula. The costs of these random solutions ranged from £96 158 to £145 298. However, the distribution of costs of these random solutions was heavily skewed towards the lower end. Nearly 90% of the solutions fell within the lower half of the overall range of costs, and well over 50% fell within the lower quarter of the overall range. Approximately 44% of the solutions fell within the range of £95 000 to £105 000, which is the range one might consider the client would be prepared to accept for this hypothetical development problem.

GDM itself produced on demand twenty-five solutions, all within the range £95 000 to £100 000. No human designers were reported as attempting the problem in order that a comparison might be made. The relevance of the data from the 1000 random solutions, however, is that it suggests that it would not have been at all difficult for a human designer to produce a low-cost solution comparable with those of the GDM. After all, there was clearly a 44% probability of producing *at random* a design of around the £100 000 cost mark. It presumably would have been quite possible for a designer to eliminate at least a little of this randomness from his intentions, so as to bring his solution below £100 000.

On the basis of what little evidence there is, designers do seem to be quite good at producing near-optimum solutions. It may be remembered that the architects in the case study that formed the basis of Luckman's (1967) AIDA design method chose a design solution which was later demonstrated by the AIDA method to be the minimum-cost solution.

Overall, then, there seems to be little reliable evidence to support an hypothesis that CAD systems are genuinely effective in improving the standard of design solutions. Even on their own terms of quantifiable measures of the built environment, their effectiveness has not been convincingly demonstrated. On other terms, such as the handling of the qualitative, the machine as yet offers no contest. There still remains an outstanding need for more rigorous research in the evaluation of computer-aided design.

8.2 Man–machine systems design

The CAD system designers are really hoist with their own petard: their design process is failing them. If computers are to be used as genuine 'aids' in the design process, then it seems clear that these new man–machine systems themselves require more careful design than they appear to have received in most cases to date. This is suggested by the very limited (or even negative) effectiveness of prototype systems in comparison with unaided designers.

Conventionally the man–machine sytems designer adopts a procedure based on the identification and specification of functions to be performed in the system, and the subsequent allocation of these functions to man or machine in accordance with relative human and machine abilities (figure 8.1). Singleton (1966) stresses that "The systems designer must think in terms of *functions*; in terms, that is, of the activities required, as opposed to the ways in which they are to be effected by components". Perhaps this advice has not always been followed in the design of CAD systems. Instead, the systems designers have thought in terms of what the machine might be able to do, and once having devised these machine functions, the human functions thereby have been implicitly allocated by omission.

Such an ad hoc approach to the allocation of functions in CAD systems might be excusable in the very early stages of development of these new systems. It is, after all, the first time that design 'systems' will have incorporated any machine components other than the simplest of mechanical aids such as the T square. Nevertheless viable CAD systems will clearly now have to be designed in a more comprehensive manner, and with the use of the skills and knowledge gained in other areas of man–machine systems design.

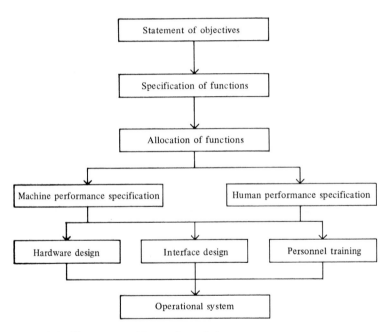

Figure 8.1. The man–machine systems design process.

8.2.1 Allocating functions

One of the simplest aids to the allocation of functions in man–machine systems design is the Fitts List (table 8.1). This is a straightforward comparison of human and machine abilities, which points up broad differences, such as human flexibility and machine rigidity. It was, however, developed originally by Fitts in 1951, and the concept of comparing human and machine abilities in this way has since been overtaken somewhat by the subsequent development of relatively highly sophisticated machines.

There is also a more fundamental criticism of the Fitts List approach. The Fitts List attempts to make essentially quantitative comparisons of humans and machines, whereas the whole point of skilled human behaviour is that it is a qualitative function. To attempt to make quantitative comparisons is to adopt a machine orientation from the outset.

This criticism is recognized and developed by Singleton (1974) in discussing the allocation of functions in man–machine systems. However, he still regards it as 'useful' to contrast the relative performance of humans and machines when considering the design of computer-aided management systems. He proposes a comparison of clerks and computers (table 8.2) which is of the Fitts List type.

The terminology used in this comparison is an indication of the attitude that still predominates in man–machine systems designing. Both human and machine attributes tend to be described in machine-like terms, so in a sense the machines have already won the 'contest' that such comparisons promote. In those comparisons human beings are not truly regarded as such, but as production 'units'. For example, see in table 8.2 the use of such comparative phrases as: "relatively cheap but cost per unit increasing".

Perhaps human beings ought to 'turn the tables' on these invidious methods of comparison. How would a poet, by contrast, compare humans and machines? Human beings did not until relatively recently tend to think of themselves in these machine terms. We did not ask, "Shall I compare thee to a summer's day—or to a versatile programmable unit?"

Table 8.1. A typical Fitts List.

	Machines	Humans
Reliability	consistent, precise	inconsistent, vague
Memory	literal, good short-term, poor access	complex, large, cross-referenced, better long-term
Reasoning	superior deductive	superior inductive
Computation	fast, accurate	slow, subject to inaccuracy
Error correction	poor	good
Judgement	objective	subjective
Evaluative abilities	quantitative	qualitative
Sensory abilities	wide range, selective, poor at pattern recognition	smaller range, subject to interference, good at pattern recognition
Manipulative abilities	limited	versatile
Programming	slow, tedious	quick, easy
Situation complexity	completely preprogrammed, can deal only with expected situations	unpredictable, can deal with unexpected situations
Overload response	sudden breakdown	gradual breakdown

Singleton (1974) shows how the 'allocation of function' concept has proceeded through an historical development. The concept began with the crude comparative assessment of *relative performance* (the Fitts List approach) in a wartime and immediately postwar environment. To this was added cost–effectiveness comparisons in the 1950s. Later the concept of the *integrated task* was developed to make rather less fragmented use of the human being's attributes, and then *graded tasks* which aimed to take advantage of the natural range in levels of human ability. Subsequently a reorientation was evident in the concept of *delegation of functions* from human to machine, with the human operator assuming a central system role. Most recently this concept has been modified into one of *flexible delegation* which involves "provision of computer facilities so that the human operator can vary his degree of participation in on-line activity and can be assisted in system prediction".

Human functions are also graded hierarchically by Singleton. At the lowest level he places *manual* functions, which can be extended by various simple tools or machines. At the next level he places *sensory* functions, which can be extended by gauges and other sensors. Next he places *decisionmaking* functions, which can be extended by information-handling devices. At the highest level he places *design* functions which he suggests can be extended by adaptive computers, although 'creativity' remains as an outstanding problem at this functional level.

The task facing the designer of computer-aided design systems is, therefore, a formidable one in that he is dealing with the highest level of human functions. Furthermore it is not sufficient merely to parcel up 'functions' into those 'best' done by computers and those 'best' done by people.

Table 8.2. Relative advantages of clerks and computers (Source: Singleton, 1974).

Clerk	Computer
Superior error detection; procedure storage; multiple access to stored material	superior speed and accuracy; literal storage
Can detect dishonesty	free from emotional responses, laziness, and dishonesty
High tolerance of ambiguity, vagueness, and uncertainty	requires precise instructions and precise evidence
Easy to program	tedious to program
Intelligent, therefore versatile	encourages fixed techniques
Available in large numbers	still relatively rare
Relatively cheap but cost per unit increasing	very expensive but cost per unit of computational power decreasing rapidly

8.2.2 Positioning the interface

Whitfield (1967) has approached the problem of allocation of functions from a consideration of human skill as the most important determinant. He suggests that the allocation of functions "can be pictured as the positioning of the interface or boundary between the human operators and the hardware of the system in terms of the relative amounts of information processing to be performed by each part. At one extreme the interface would be very close to the hardware, leaving the operator to perform extensive manipulation of information received from, or to be sent to, the equipment; at the other extreme the interface would be close to the operator in that his tasks would be relatively undemanding."

This seems to summarize well the situation in CAD systems design, where, as we have seen in the experiments of chapter 5, the interface in some prototype systems appears to be positioned too close to the hardware, in that the human operator has to cope with large amounts of confusing information. On the other hand, it would not be desirable to shift the interface too close to the operator, so as to leave him with only trivial tasks to perform. As well as dehumanizing the design process, this latter error could also *re*mystify it, so that only the computer would seem to 'know' how to design.

This error has crept into some of the 'participatory' CAD systems which attempt to provide a 'naive' designer—the layman—with a computer facility that will enable him to design, say, a house. Here the design facility is often exclusively retained by the machine, which therefore requests only some crude initial input information from its user (usually on desired room relationships) before producing its design to these requirements. The user is denied any access to the actual design process, and the machine behaves like any other 'automat' machine. Human and machine roles are crudely unbalanced.

The ludicrous heights to which this kind of CAD program can rise have been well demonstrated by Gero and Julian (1975) of the University of Sydney. Their on-line 'Interactive Design' program adopts a totally dominant role and a style of output chat that is by turns friendly, bullying, or as vigorously matey as perhaps only an Australian computer could be. It demands to know your full name, then insists on addressing you by your Christian name as though you and it were old friends. It rewards your simplest correct input with a "BEAUTY!" or "BONZA!" It will rap your knuckles (only metaphorically, so far) for typing "HELP" at an inappropriate moment, with the admonition: "THERE IS NO ASSISTANCE HERE, JUST ANSWER THE QUESTION". It will only very reluctantly let you end the rather one-sided conversation it has been having with you: "WARREN, ARE YOU SURE THAT YOU DESIRE TO FINISH?" It will indeed design a house for you, but in a most mystifying manner, somewhere deep inside its manic circuitry.

A mechanistic approach to allocating functions and positioning interfaces is being challenged in the CAAD field only by the work of Negroponte (1975) and his colleagues, in their attempts to create 'soft' architecture machines which try to ignore the conventional boundaries to 'machine attributes'. The basic situation in current human–machine relationships, and the radical alternative, is highlighted by Jungk (1976) in his question: "is it possible to construct machines which actually respond to the human rhythm, rather than the human being responding to the rhythm of the machine?"

8.3 The allocation of roles

Vaughan and Schumacher-Mavor (1972) have criticized human factors specialists for being slow to develop new aids to systems design much beyond the Fitts List, particularly in respect of systems that incorporate computers. They suggest that "computer technology has advanced rapidly, while human engineering and system engineering specialists have failed to shift from a man versus machine task allocation orientation to a man-with-a-computer concept for accomplishing cognitive work".

One of the major difficulties that hinder progress in this field of man–computer role formulation is that 'cognitive work' is not itself an established, static concept. The role that a computer can play in a problem-solving system will depend on what is known about how to solve the particular problems that the system is designed for. In this respect, the original perceptive insight of Lady Lovelace in reference to Babbage's Analytical Engine in the mid-nineteenth century still holds: a computer can do "whatever we know how to order it to perform".

This is essentially the same point as that made by Newell (1965); that the mode of problem-solving (whether algorithmic or heuristic) is determined by the current state of knowledge about that particular problem type. If it is known 'how to solve' a type of problem, then an algorithm is developed for it, and hence that type of problem-solving can reliably be incorporated into the computer's role. If it is not known 'how to solve it', beyond giving it to a human problem-solver, then the problem type has, by definition, to be solved heuristically.

8.3.1 Strategies and tactics

Michie et al (1968) reinforce this point in discussion of their experiments comparing man versus man–machine versus machine abilities at solving problems of the 'travelling salesman' type. The man–machine combination should, they suggest, "be regarded as a means of forcing entry into territory which would be otherwise impenetrable, but which it is intended ultimately to subjugate to the arts of full mechanization. We thus see interactive graphics not as an end in themselves but as a step towards having the problem solved entirely by the machine behind the scenes. We see a progression of stages.... What is strategic today is tactical tomorrow".

In the light of the above review, of the need for a more careful consideration of human and machine roles, this statement by Michie et al appears too sweeping. However, it does emphasize that the state of knowledge about problem solving is constantly evolving. This, in turn, means that machine 'abilities' are also constantly evolving. The systems designer must therefore start with something that is more constant, that is with human abilities, and seek to complement these abilities with machine functions where, when, and if the latter are relevant.

What is known about some aspects of human abilities in decisionmaking has been summarized by Vaughan and Schumacher-Mavor (1972). Their summary points seem to have much in common with what might be deduced from the behaviour of the subjects using the interactive computer mode in the experiments of chapter 5. Of the typical decisionmaker Vaughan and Schumacher-Mavor say: "He is a generally poor diagnostician and does not learn by exposure to complex tasks but only when specific relationships that make up the complexity are explained. He is not particularly inventive and tends to adopt the first solution he develops. He finds it difficult to use more than one criterion at a time in evaluating actions and tends only to identify criteria that reflect favourably on the action he is developing."

8.3.2 System design concept

The conclusion reached by Vaughan and Schumacher-Mavor on a man–computer systems design concept is somewhat different from most others that have been developed. They say: "The emerging structure of the man–computer, conversationally interactive system concept is that man directs, via guidelines, goals and constraints; the computer generates hypotheses and alternatives; man selects out those to be developed; the computer tests; and the man evaluates the results of the tests. The computer opens up and widens both the problem and the solution space; the man evaluates and narrows it down."

There is also considerable common ground here with the findings of Levin (1966a; 1966b) from his observations of designers at work. The relevant points of Levin's analysis may be summarized as: the designer needs to learn about the given problem by exposing conflicts and building up specific relationships; the designer needs to generate a wide variety of solutions; the designer needs to incorporate a range of (other people's) criteria in evaluating a proposed solution. These needs are generated by the nature of the design task and by the limitations of human abilities in attempting that task. Perhaps here, then, are the starting points for CAD systems designers.

Questions for design systems

9.1 The design of design

The initial difficulty facing any systems designer is in determining the overall system specification, or 'statement of objectives' (see figure 8.1, page 134). Unless this specification is set by some arbitrary limitation, by the client commissioning the system design, or by some other external means, the designer usually finds it extremely difficult to decide just where the boundaries of his problem lie. As Singleton (1974) says, "One general difficulty about translating the systems philosophy into practice is in the identification of the boundaries of the system under consideration. The origin of this problem is in the inherent hierarchical nature of systems. Every system is made up of other systems and is itself a component of a larger system." The system designer tends to find it enticingly, but frustratingly, easy to conclude that his system objectives could better be met by redesigning the next system up the hierarchy, and so on.

The same enticement and frustration faces the designer of a design system. Why stop at the level of the architect's design process? Surely the problems would be better solved by redesigning the whole commission and design process? Even better by redesigning the commission and design and construction processes?

9.1.1 What is designing?

Eventually, of course, *some* level has to be decided on. But even if one is prepared to settle for the fairly obvious level of the design process itself—for example, from brief to detail design—the problem of deciding the system objectives still remains. What are the objectives of a design system? The overall objective must be 'to design'. But what is 'to design'?

'To design' is to tackle a unique type of problem. Design problems are not like scientific, mathematical, or logical problems, which generally require the 'proof' of an hypothesis. They are not like crossword puzzles or guessing games, which have a single correct answer. They are not like the problems of an artist or a composer, who works principally to satisfy self-imposed goals and standards. Design problems often contain aspects of all these other types of problem, whilst remaining distinct.

To illustrate something of the nature of what it is 'to design', let us consider a range of definitions. These definitions can vary from attempts to be methodical, such as "a goal-directed, problem-solving activity" (Archer, 1965); or managerial, as in "the conscious effort to impose meaningful order" (Papanek, 1972); to the frankly mystical: "the performing of a very complicated act of faith" (Jones, 1966). Let us consider each of these definitions in turn.

A goal-directed, problem-solving activity. Now, although design activity must indeed be directed towards a goal, it is often the case that subgoals, and occasionally the overall goal, of a design problem will be changed as the problem is explored. Goals can therefore only be *fixed* after a certain amount of problem exploration. This in turn means that 'to design' is not solely 'to problem-solve'; to some extent it is also 'to problem-find'. It is only by exploring the details of the general problem as given, often as exposed by considering tentative solutions, that the designer can find the critical problems and subproblems that need to be resolved.

The conscious effort to impose meaningful order. This definition is called into question by the use of the word 'meaningful', just as the previous definition inadequately dealt with goals. What is 'meaningful'? To whom, at what point in time, and under what circumstances is a solution going to be meaningful? There are important questions of values in designing, that this definition implies, but skates over. It also places an explicit stress on 'conscious effort'. Does this mean that subconscious or even unconscious effort is inadmissable? Can a designer not literally 'dream up' a solution? It would surely be foolish to reject good solutions just because they did not have a thorough pedigree of conscious effort. Since 'to design' undeniably involves creative activity, the designer often has to rely on the somewhat mysterious workings of the creative human brain at both conscious and subconscious levels.

The performing of a very complicated act of faith. This definition says little more than that no one knows how or why design activity actually works. The designer is often working in the dark, uncertain of the direction in which to move and of what will be the outcome of his actions. It is therefore with much 'faith' that he begins and continues 'to design'. But to rely on somehow being able to 'muddle through' in the hope that something will turn up by way of a solution would in most cases be rather foolish. Instead, the designer must prepare some strategy, or planned sequence of actions, and must inevitably review that strategy from time to time—particularly if it does not seem to be producing the goods, that is, identifying the right problems and generating suitable solutions.

Each of the definitions considered above contains some truth about what it is 'to design', but no single one of them contains all the truth. Even taken together as a set they leave out some important aspects. So perhaps no simple definition can contain the complexity of the nature of design.

9.1.2 Magic versus hackwork

If answers to the question 'What is designing?' remain so enigmatic (and this is not to say that they always should or will), then how is the designer of a design system to define his objectives? In practice, design system designers tend, naturally enough, to wade as briskly as possible through the swamps of enigma onto firmer ground. They follow the advice of system-design strategists such as Miller (1969), who divides the activity of design into two distinct processes: one being the origination of a 'design principle', and the other being the translation of that principle into 'an actuality'.

Miller explains the distinction thus: "The concept of the Guggenheim Museum as a vertical corkscrew which enables all the pictures in an exhibit to be displayed on one unwinding corridor is an example of the concept of a design principle. The discovery or extrapolation, or plagiarism, of the design principle is not relevant to treatment here. At least temporarily, regard the happening of the design concept or principle as an act of magic.... But the arduous activity of translating a design concept into a symbolic statement of the construction itself is relevant here. The designer, having fallible memory, may need to be reminded of the size of the land plot, the statutes covering water facilities in the building being designed, the limits of structural strength in a given supporting mass of concrete, the maximum amperes that can be imposed on a given circuit material, the strength of the rock under a footing, and so on."

Computers cannot cope (yet) with the 'magic' aspects of design, argues Miller, but they can assist with the more mundane aspects. And "let it be acknowledged, in a quiet undertone, that a huge amount of what is called 'design' is hackwork". On such an assumption, that designing can be subdivided into 'magic' and 'hackwork', rests the design of many computer-aided design systems. Yet, expressed so crudely, surely no designer would agree that such a subdivision can be made? Designing is much more of a holistic activity than this.

The subdivision of designing into 'magic' and 'hackwork' is both mistaken and dangerous. The danger is that the CAD systems which deal in hackwork will come to dominate the design process, and the 'magic' will be forgotten. The system boundary will have been drawn too narrowly, for the sake of short-term convenience, and in the long term what was left outside the boundary will be ignored and will atrophy.

9.1.3 The power of the system designer

In drawing boundaries, the system designer is in the powerful position of recognizing or ignoring various facets and criteria of the whole system under consideration. "And so it is", comments Boguslaw (1965), "that a designer of systems, who has the de facto prerogative to specify the range of phenomena that his system will distinguish, clearly is in possession of enormous degrees of power". Boguslaw is referring more to large-scale sociotechnical systems such as traffic management, crime detection, or education, rather than to smaller systems such as CAD. However, his comment on the system designer's prerogative "to specify the range of phenomena" is pertinent at all levels of systems design.

In fact, Boguslaw addresses his remarks particularly to the problems of system designs that incorporate computers. The very nature of computer operations means that "the world of reality must at some point in time be reduced to binary form", a reduction which has some inherent limitations. The circuitry of the computer, the structure of the language used to communicate with the computer, and the computer programmer himself, all place a stringent set of restrictions on the alternatives and possibilities that may be treated in a computer-based system.

"It is in this sense", Boguslaw says, "that computer programmers, the designers of computer equipment, and the developers of computer languages possess power. To the extent that decisions made by each of these participants in the design process serve to reduce, limit or totally eliminate action alternatives, they are applying force and wielding power in the precise sociological meaning of these terms." The systems designer exercises his power through permitting only a certain range of actions as valid in his system; *permission* for a range of actions always implies *prohibition* of alternative actions.

Roszak (1972) makes a further, scathing attack on systems analysis. He quotes the systems expert Simon Ramo's definition of a good systems design team, which is that it "combines individuals who have specialised variously in mathematics, physics, chemistry, other branches of physical science, psychology, sociology, business finance, government, and so on". Roszak then comments, "Notably, the good systems team does not include poets, painters, holy men or social revolutionaries, who, presumably, have nothing to contribute to 'real-life solutions'".

9.1.4 The design of design systems

These ethical doubts about systems designing may seem rather abstruse, but they certainly do have practical implications for the users of systems that might be coarsely, simplistically, and bureaucratically designed. These users (in our case, the users of computer-aided design systems) may not have much choice as to whether or not to use such restrictive systems, or may be unaware of the inherent restrictions and coercions of the systems.

These problems of the design of design systems have been badly neglected in the past decade of development of CAD systems. There is, however, little excuse for such neglect. The problems were clearly set out at the 1962 Conference on Design Methods by Esherick (1963), in terms of a set of questions:

Are quantitative approaches to design likely to be restrictive or limiting? Are they likely to be authoritarian or dictatorial?

Are they likely to produce a monolithic social order or one so strongly structured and framed that there is no freedom of movement or choice?

Are quantitative approaches to design likely to generate systems which will ultimately become closed systems in spite of every effort to keep them open, forcing upon us a formalistic design process insensitive to the demands of a living and growing human system and leading to a fixed and rigid environment?

Esherick was not asking such questions purely rhetorically, in the assumption that the answer to each was 'Yes', and that, therefore, quantitative approaches to design should be eschewed. Rather, as he himself said, "These questions are asked in the hope that one of the central purposes in the design of a design system will be to give in reply to these questions a firm 'No!'" The questions still need to be asked, with still the same hope.

The users of CAD systems—the architects and other designers—must develop and maintain an awareness of the implications that these systems hold for them, their work and their objectives. They must anticipate and interpret the role of the computer as that role develops. Machines are not introduced into industry and commerce in a motivational vacuum, but in a social, economic, and political context of motivations. It is within such a context that the imminent allocation of human and machine roles in design will be resolved.

9.2 System checklist

We have seen that computer-aided architectural design is being developed and implemented in a generally ad hoc, piecemeal fashion, and that these developments are usually poorly evaluated and assessed for either their effectiveness or their effects on the designer and the design process. We have also seen that the 'threats' and 'promises' of computer-aided architectural design are equally matched, and that not enough attention is being paid to the very real and serious aspects of the 'threats' side of the matter. Yet it also seems likely that the implementation of CAAD systems will grow and spread; before long, large-scale comprehensive systems will be being introduced in architectural practice—probably, in the first instance, in Government and other public design offices.

What seems to be needed, in addition to more rigorous research, evaluation, and assessment, and in addition to more careful systems design for human roles, is a fairly straightforward, generalized assessment procedure that can be used both by architects and by CAD systems designers in a joint exercise at the start of any proposed implementation of a comprehensive CAAD system. It is with such a purpose in mind that the following CAAD System Checklist is proposed. Being a first attempt at such a checklist, it is inevitably a simple one and will need refinement in the light of experience. However, if architects and systems designers can evolve mutually satisfactory answers to the questions raised in the Checklist, then the automated architect might indeed transpire as a promise fulfilled, rather than as a threat imposed.

CAAD system checklist
System design
How will the particular computer system be chosen?
    What criteria will be used to select a system?
    Who will be responsible for deciding on the particular system?
    Who will be consulted?
Who are the system designers?
    What is their experience and background?
What are the objectives of the system?
    What is it meant to achieve?
    Why is it being implemented?
What functions will the system perform?
    Does it replace existing functions of the design office?
    Does it change existing functions?
    Does it ignore some existing functions? If so, what will happen to those
    functions?
How will system functions be selected?
    What programs or other aids will be incorporated?
    Who will decide on system functions? With what criteria?
    How will functions be updated or otherwise modified in the light of
    experience and further developments?

Human factors
What ergonomic or human factors attention has been paid to the design of
the 'interfaces' between computer and architect?
    Are the input data relatively easy to prepare and present to the computer?
    What forms does the output take? Is it readily understandable?
    Does the output genuinely aid decisionmaking in design?

Personnel
Who will immediately be affected by the implementation of the system,
and in what ways?
    Have these people been consulted? What is their reaction?
Who will operate the system?
    What training will they need?
    What work pattern will they be required to adopt?
Who will be barred from operating the system?
    Will this be because of lack of training, or by explicit ruling, or by
    system design and accessibility?
Who will be responsible for the 'machine minding' tasks?
    Who will punch cards and tapes?
    Who will write programs?
    Who will deal with errors and breakdowns?

Efficiency

What is the expected increase in efficiency of the design process—that is, what reduction in man-hours is predicted?

Has the predicted time saving been tested?

Where do the savings occur?

What other savings have been assumed in order to make the system justifiable and viable?

Employment

What effect is the computer system expected to have on employment?

Will there be a reduced need for design staff?

Who will be affected?

Office organization

How will the design office be restructured to incorporate the computer system?

What will be a normal project team?

How will it be organized?

How will teams change from project to project?

How will the management structure of the office change and adapt?

Will there be changes in the responsibilities held by members of the office?

Will the management 'pyramid' be affected?

Will promotion prospects be affected?

Building team organization

How will the work of other members of the building team—quantity surveyors, engineers, etc—be affected by the computer system?

Who will have access to which files?

How will information swapping between files be coordinated?

What will be the team structure with the new system?

Working pressure

How much of the designer's working day will be spent working on-line with the computer?

Are on-line periods of intensive work fairly brief and separated by longer periods of a more relaxed pace?

What other steps will be taken to reduce the expected stress of computer-paced work?

Who will have access to records of the designer's work with the computer?

Will there be someone 'looking over the designer's shoulder', checking his decisionmaking records?

What will be the filing system for keeping records?

Design process
What structure for the design process does the computer system assume and impose?
    On what model of the design activity is the system based?
    What structure to design problems does it assume?
    What approach to design and problemsolving does it require its user to adopt?

Design solutions
What constraints will the computer system impose on the kinds of buildings that can be designed?
    Will it accept a particular building system, or a few systems, only?
    What limitations are there on the shapes, forms, and arrangements that it can handle?

Relations with clients and other users
How will the computer system affect the designer's relationship with the project client and the building users?
    Will the client and/or users have access to the computer data and outputs?
    Will they be able to participate in the computer-aided design process?
    Will the computer system tend to 'democratize' or to 'bureaucratize' the design process?

Appendix

A guide to computer applications in architectural design. Systems discussed in the text are marked•.

Program or system name and references	Description
ARK 2 Lee and Stewart (1972) Renfrow (1976) Stewart and Lee (1971)	A comprehensive CAAD system developed by USA architectural practice of Perry, Dean and Stewart. Component programs include: COMPROGRAPH—analysis of current and future space needs of the client, data file of space schedules for project; COMPROPLAN—synthesis of spatial layout based on functional relationships; bubble diagrams and block layouts are generated and can be manipulated on CRT display. COMPROSPACE—individual room-design aid based on typical furniture, etc, layouts. COMPROVIEW—perspective drawings.
•BAID (Basic Architectural Investigation and Design) Auger (1972)	An aid to the design of medium-rise high-density housing schemes. Site planning controls based on requirements of daylight, sunlight, and privacy (distance between houses) are applied as constraints on the location of houses. The program generates a site layout by randomly selecting possible locations that are within the constraints. It can also be used to check the viability of site layouts produced manually.
BIBRACS (Brockhouse Integrated Building Realisation and Construction) Mountford (1974)	For implementation with CLASP and similar component building systems. Produces production, etc information from a detail design fed into the computer by the building designer. Computer outputs include coded elevation drawings, coded floor plans, coded steel-frame drawings, foundation plans, Bills of Quantities, schedules, etc. The computer also reports on error conditions found in the designer's input data.
BOP (Building Optimization Program) Graham (1969)	Developed by USA architectural practice of Skidmore, Owings and Merrill, for use in the design of commercial office buildings. Given basic constraints on site, height, lease, span, floor area, etc limits, the program indicates the possible solutions in terms of number of storeys, dimensions, etc, with calculations of total building costs, returns on investment, percentage of rentable floor area, cost m^{-2}, etc. Selected solutions can then be examined in more detail, including mechanical, electrical, etc services requirements, structural dimensions, optimum lift configurations, etc. Standard floor plans and elevations can also be drawn by the computer.

Appendix (continued)

Program or system name and references	Description
•CEDAR (Computer-aided Environmental Design Analysis and Realisation) Chalmers (1972)	Developed by a research group in the Property Services Agency (PSA) of the Department of the Environment and intended for implementation in PSA design offices. The prototype CEDAR system was based on the design requirements of Post Office Telephone Engineering Centre buildings in the SEAC building system, although it is now thought to be generally applicable to any building type, provided the SEAC system is still used. CEDAR will provide a comprehensive CAD system for the PSA architects, from sketch design stage to detail design, structural analysis, and the production of working drawings and schedules. It is intended to relieve the designer of 'tedious' design tasks.
•City-Scape Kamnitzer (1969)	Based on NASA visual-simulation systems, and provides a moving, coloured, perspective CRT image of a simulated drive or walk through an architectural landscape. The direction, speed, and angle of vision at all points of the simulated trip are controlled by the viewer. Architectural details of the early versions of City-Scape were limited to simple block models, but the system could be extended to greater sophistication.
•CLUSTER Milne (1970)	Intended principally for use in education, as a teaching aid in environmental problem-solving. The program identifies the interconnected subsets of a set of planning elements. It gives information on decomposition and recomposition of the subsets, indicating the relationships between subproblems of the overall design task, and its network-like structure.
•COPLANNER (Computer-oriented Planning) Souder et al (1964)	A pioneering CAAD system, sponsored by the American Hospital Association. On the basis of movement ('commerce') data, the system allows a designer to study the interaction of building layout and commerce pattern. Bar-charts of data are used as the principal means of expressing the commerce patterns, displayed on a CRT. The program simulates commerce in the proposed hospital, over a typical twenty-four-hour period.

F

Appendix (continued)

Program or system name and references	*Description*
CRAFT (Computerized Relative Allocation of Facilities Technique) Buffa et al (1964) Lew and Brown (1970)	Originally developed for aiding the design of industrial plant layouts, but has been adapted to spatial-arrangement problems in architecture. The program starts from any given layout or spatial arrangement, for which it calculates the overall layout 'cost' in terms of distances, journey frequencies, and journey weightings between each pair of components in the layout. It then proceeds to swap the location of pairs or trios of components, and recalculates the overall 'cost' after each swap. This procedure continues until no further improvement is found possible, thus producing an assumed optimum or near-optimum solution.
CRAFT-3D Cinar (1975)	An extension of CRAFT which enables the program to deal with multi-storey (three-dimensional) layouts.
DISCOURSE Porter et al (1970)	A program for manipulating data in city-planning problems. It handles a variety of information (population, land-use, etc) about a geographic area, and rules for how the information is transformed. The designer can store, retrieve, and modify this information, and use it to explore planning policies or the effects of environmental changes. The information is displayed either in lists or in a map format.
•GDM (General Decision Model) Berger et al (1974) Gill and Berger (1972)	This on-going research aims to apply work in machine intelligence to the problems of architectural design. The GDM contains an heuristic program which attempts to optimize a building envelope within sets of both specific and general design constraints. It starts with a simple geometric shape and gradually alters and refines this within the boundaries and relationships set by the constraints such as the relationships between required floor area, site limits, building dimensions, number of storeys, etc. The program's own 'learning' about the problem is meant to play a fundamental role in the overall model.
• Harness Meager (1972) Radford (1974)	A building design system for hospitals in which standardized departments are arranged around a 'Harness zone' of circulation. Associated CAD programs include both synthesis and evaluation of such plan arrangements.

Appendix (continued)

Program or system name and references	Description
●HIDECS (Hierarchical Decomposition of Sets) Alexander and Manheim (1962)	The pioneering, but subsequently little-used program developed for Alexander's (1963; 1964) method of decomposing the set of individual components of a design problem into independent subsets which are strongly connected internally. The program takes a matrix covering the potential interactions between each pair of components, and produces lists of the components which form the subsets.
●IMAGE Weinzapfel and Handel (1975) Weinzapfel and Johnson (1972)	This system deals with the manipulation of physical design elements—usually the rooms to be provided in a building. The designer specifies the set of elements in his problem to the computer, together with relationships between, and constraints on, the elements—such as whether a pair of elements should be near or far apart, be on the same floor level, have visual access between them, be of a certain size, etc. IMAGE can then generate layouts either automatically or through interaction with the designer by means of a CRT display. The intention is not to generate an 'optimum' layout, but to help and encourage the designer to explore a variety of possible solutions. Layouts are evaluated by the IMAGE system in terms of a ranking and testing of the worst situations occurring in the layout and the criteria affecting those situations.
●MDS (Multidimensional scaling) Kernohan et al (1971)	Converts numerical data on proximity relationships between elements into a spatial configuration based on the relative strengths of the relationships. The output can be in multidimensional 'space', but only two or three dimensional outputs are normally relevant to architectural design.
OXSYS (Oxford System) Hoskins (1972; 1973) Richens (1974)	A comprehensive system applied to the Oxford-method component building system for hospitals. OXSYS starts from a sketch design prepared by the designer, and a brief containing details of the hospital departments, rooms, and their performance requirements. The sketch is developed into a detailed design in a partly automatic, partly manual fashion by the designer inputting, for example, the location of structural components and directions of spans, which allows the computer then to select the appropriate components from the building system. Performance evaluations—for example of daylighting and thermal performance—can be obtained, enabling the designer to experiment with and test different configurations and types of wall cladding, etc. Working drawings, schedules, etc are produced by the computer.

Appendix (continued)

Program or system name and references	*Description*
•PACE (Package for Architectural Computer Evaluation) Maver (1971)	An interactive computer program which provides a set of performance evaluations of any building at preliminary design stage. The designer describes the outline design in terms of simple departmental or room blocks, and the program responds with evaluations of such criteria as capital, maintenance, and running costs; heating, lighting, and ventilation requirements; site utilization; spatial arrangements, etc.
•SPACES (Scheduling Package, and Computer Evaluation for Schools) Th'ng and Davies (1975)	This is a 'suite' of programs —SPACES 1, SPACES 2, and SPACES 3—which operates in the context of the sketch design of school buildings with the use of a component building system such as CLASP. The three programs are relevant to the design stages of analysis, synthesis, and evaluation, respectively. SPACES 1 is concerned with determining the schedule of accommodation for the school, and provides a much 'tighter' schedule than is conventionally compiled manually by more closely scrutinizing the actual spatial requirements of the school timetable. SPACES 2 is concerned with the block layout of the building. It generates a 'bubble' diagram based on functional relationships between blocks, which can be manipulated on the CRT by the designer, and then converted to a rectilinear representation. SPACES 3 subjects the layout to an evaluation of its economic, functional, environmental, etc performance.
SSHA/Edinburgh Bijl (1974) Bijl and Shawcross (1975)	This system has been developed for the Scottish Special Housing Association by Edinburgh University. One aspect is concerned with the site layout of housing estates. The program assists the design of such layouts by calculating three-dimensional alignments of roads, etc from a two-dimensional plan, drainage plans, and house floor levels. Another aspect of the system is concerned with individual house design, and is applicable to any standardized form of construction. It provides structural, floor area, daylight, etc calculations, and produces working drawings, schedules, etc.
•STUNI (Stirling University) Willoughby (1970) Willoughby et al (1970)	Developed at Strathclyde University as part of an exercise for the design of Stirling University. This program generates a layout of departments on a gridded site plan, on the basis of two criteria—site conditions (a value for each grid location) and interdepartmental relationships (a value for the strength of relationships between each pair of departments). The layout can be two- or three-dimensional.

Appendix (continued)

Program or system name and references	*Description*
●URBAN5 Negroponte (1970) Negroponte and Groisser (1970)	An interactive graphics system, developed as an exercise in 'conversing' with a machine about environmental design projects. The designer builds on the CRT display an outline three-dimensional arrangement of standard cubes. He can specify relationships between cubes, conditions that attach to them, etc. The machine continually evaluates the design proposal against these criteria and provides this evaluation on request or sometimes by 'interrupting' the designer. The system was meant to adapt itself to the designer, becoming a design 'partner'.
●West Sussex Paterson (1974) Peters (1972) Ray-Jones (1968)	This comprehensive system was developed in the West Sussex County Architect's Department. The designer interacts with the computer through a CRT display, and the computer constantly revises its model of the building being designed, as the designer creates and modifies it. The computer provides a file of standard components and performance evaluations of the proposed design. When the design is complete, it produces working drawings, schedules, etc.
●Whitehead and Eldars Whitehead (1970) Whitehead and Eldars (1964; 1965)	A classic program, which takes as input an association matrix representing values for the relationships between each pair of elements (for example, rooms, departments) in the building-design problem. By building up from the most strongly related pair, the program creates an 'optimum' layout.

References

Each reference which is included in the classified bibliography is indicated by the letter corresponding to the section in which it appears.

Adams J, Cohen L, 1969 "Time-sharing versus instant batch-processing: an experiment in programmer training" *Computers and Automation* **18** (3) 30-34

I Alexander C, 1963 "The determination of components for an Indian village" in *Conference on Design Methods* Eds J C Jones, D Thornley (Pergamon Press, Oxford), pp 83-114

Alexander C, 1964 *Notes on the Synthesis of Form* (Harvard University Press, Cambridge, Mass.)

F Alexander C, 1965 "The question of computers in design" *Landscape* (Spring), 6-8

Alexander C, 1966 "A city is not a tree" *Design* **206** 46-55

F Alexander C, 1971 "The state of the art in design methods" *DMG Newsletter* **5** (3) 3-7 [Reprinted in *DMG-DRS Journal* **7** (2) 133-135, 1973]

J Alexander C, Manheim M, 1962 "HIDECS 2: a computer program for the hierarchical decomposition of a set with an associated graph" Civil Engineering Systems Laboratory Publication 160, Massachusetts Institute of Technology, Cambridge, Mass.

H Applied Research of Cambridge, 1973 *Computer Aided Building: A Study of Current Trends* (Applied Research of Cambridge, Cambridge, England)

Archer L B, 1965 *Systematic Method for Designers* (The Design Council, London)

Archer L B, 1972 "Computers, design theory and the handling of the qualitative" *Proceedings of the International Conference on Computers in Architecture, York* (British Computer Society, London)

Architecture Machine Group, 1971 "Computer aids to participatory architecture" National Science Foundation Proposal, Architecture Machine Group, Massachusetts Institute of Technology, Cambridge, Mass.

Asimow M, 1962 *Introduction to Design* (Prentice-Hall, Englewood Cliffs, NJ)

A Auger B, 1972 *The Architect and the Computer* (Pall Mall Press, London)

Bazjanac V, 1972 "On the uses of computer-aided models in design" paper presented at the Architect Researchers' Conference Los Angeles (American Institute of Architects, Los Angeles, Calif.)

Beaumont M J, 1967 *Computer-aided Techniques for Synthesis of Layout and Form with Respect to Circulation* unpublished PhD Thesis, University of Bristol, Bristol, England

Bell D, 1967 "Notes on the post-industrial society" *The Public Interest* Part 6 (Winter), 24-35 [Extracts reprinted in Cross N, Elliott D, Roy R (Eds), 1974 *Man-made Futures* (Hutchinson, London) pp 99-106]

Bell D, 1974 *The Coming of Post-Industrial Society* (Heinemann, London)

J Berger S R, Briggs M P, Gill R, Markovits N, 1974 *The Construction and Extension of a General Decision Model and its Application to Space-Planning problems* Department of Architecture, University of Bristol, Bristol, England (mimeo)

H Bijl A, 1974 "Research in progress: Edinburgh CAAD studies" *Computer Aided Design* **6** (3) 183-186

I Bijl A, Shawcross G, 1975 "Housing site layout system" *Computer Aided Design* **7** (1) 2-10

Boguslaw R, 1965 *The New Utopians* (Prentice-Hall, Englewood Cliffs, NJ)

Broadbent G, 1966 "Design method in architecture" *The Architects' Journal* 14 September, 679-685

Broadbent G (1968) "A plain man's guide to systematic design methods" *RIBA Journal* May, 223-227

A Broadbent G, 1973 *Design in Architecture* (John Wiley, Chichester)

Broadbent G, Ward A (Eds), 1969 *Design Methods in Architecture* (Lund Humphries, London)

I Buffa E S, Armour G C, Vollman T E, 1964 "Allocating facilities with CRAFT" *Harvard Business Review* **42** (2) 136-158

Building Economics Research Unit, 1968 "Pilot study of the building timetable: third progress report" University College London, Environmental Research Group (mimeo)

Building Research Station, 1969 *A Study of Coding and Data Co-ordination for the Building Industry* (HMSO, London)

Cakin S, 1976 *Evaluation and Participation in Design* unpublished PhD Thesis, University of Strathclyde, Glasgow, Scotland

A Campion D, 1968 *Computers in Architectural Design* (Elsevier, London)

Carbonell J R, Elkind J, Nickerson R, 1968 "On the psychological importance of time in a time-sharing system" *Human Factors* **10** 135-142

Chalmers J, 1972 "The development of CEDAR" in *Proceedings of the International Conference on Computers in Architecture, York* (British Computer Society, London) pp 126-140

Chermayeff S, Alexander C, 1963 *Community and Privacy* (Doubleday, Garden City, NY) [Reprinted by Penguin, Harmondsworth (1966)]

Cinar U, 1975 "Facilities planning: a systems analysis and space allocation approach" in *Spatial Synthesis in Computer-Aided Building Design* Ed. C M Eastman (Applied Science Publishers, London) pp 19-40

I Coleman J R, 1973 "Computer aids for participation in housing design" *Computer Aided Design* **5** (3) 166-170

Cooley M, 1972 "Computer-aided design: its nature and implications" Amalgamated Union of Engineering Workers, Technical and Supervisory Section, Richmond, Surrey

Cooley M, 1973 "Dialectics of the man-machine interaction" paper presented at The Design Activity International Conference, London (Design Research Society)

Cross N, 1967 *Simulation of Computer-Aided Design* unpublished MSc dissertation, University of Manchester Institute of Science and Technology, Manchester, England

G Cross N, 1972a "Impact of computers on the architectural design process" *The Architects' Journal* 22 March, 623-628

D Cross N (Ed.), 1972b *Design participation—Proceedings of the Design Research Society Conference, Manchester* (Academy Editions, London)

Cross N, 1972c "Predicting the effects of computer-aided design systems" *Proceedings of the International Conference on Computers in Architecture, York* (British Computer Society, London) pp 157-166

J Cross N, Eastham L, Morton M, 1970 "Computer-aided information retrieval: a pilot study of some possibilities" *Building* 11 September, 127-131

Cross N, Maver T W, 1970 "User experience: time-sharing terminals" *Bulletin of Computer-Aided Architectural Design* **2** 5-7

F Cross N, Maver T W, 1973 "Computer aids for design participation" *Architectural Design* May, 274

Davies M, 1975 *A Computer-Aided Architectural Design Approach to Secondary School Design* unpublished PhD Thesis volume 2, University of Strathclyde, Glasgow, Scotland

Davis R M, 1966 "Man-machine communication" *Annual Review of Information Science and Technology* **1** 221-254

G Department of the Environment, 1969 *Computer-Aided Architectural Design* (Department of the Environment, London)

Derbyshire M E, 1975 "Quantitative techniques in the preparation of a brief for a school design—a case study" *Environment and Planning B* **2** (1) 107-117

B Eastman C M (Ed.), 1975 *Spatial Synthesis in Computer-Aided Building Design* (Applied Science Publishers, London)

Eberhard J P, 1970 "We ought to know the difference" in *Emerging Methods in Environmental Design and Planning* Ed. G Moore (MIT Press, Cambridge, Mass.) pp 363–367

Ellul J, 1964 *The Technological Society* (Knopf, New York)

Erikson W J, 1966 "A pilot study of interactive vs. non-interactive debugging" SDC paper TM-3296, System Development Corporation, Santa Monica, Calif.

Esher, Lord, Llewellyn-Davies, Lord, 1968 "The architect in 1988" *RIBA Journal* October, 448–455

Esherick J, 1963 "Problems of the design of a design system" in *Conference on Design Methods* Eds J C Jones, D Thornley (Pergamon Press, Oxford) pp 75–81

Evans B, 1969 *Intelligent Computer-Aided Design Systems* unpublished MSc dissertation, University of Manchester Institute of Science and Technology, Manchester, England

Fano R M, 1965 "The MAC system: a progress report" in *Computer Augmentation of Human Reasoning* Eds M Sass, W Wilkinson (Spartan Books, Washington, DC) pp 131–150

Galbraith J K, 1967 *The New Industrial State* (Hamish Hamilton, London)

Gero J S, Julian W G, 1975 "Interaction in the planning of buildings" in *Spatial Synthesis in Computer-Aided Building Design* Ed. C M Eastman (Applied Science Publishers, London) pp 184–229

Gibbon M, Voyer R, 1973 "Techology assessment: bias free analysis" *New Scientist* 24 May, 468–450

Gill R, Berger S, 1972 "Creativity and computers" in *Proceedings of the International Conference on Computers in Architecture, York* (British Computer Society, London) pp 210–217

Gold M, 1967 *Methodology for Evaluating Time-shared Computer Usage* unpublished PhD Thesis, Massachusetts Institute of Technology, Cambridge, Mass.

Goodman R, 1972 *After the Planners* (Penguin, Harmondsworth)

G Graham B, 1969 "Computer graphics in architectural practice" in *Computer Graphics in Architecture and Design* Ed. M Milne (Yale University School of Art and Architecture, New Haven, Conn.) pp 23–30

Grant E E, Sackman H, 1967 "An exploratory investigation of programmer performance under on-line and off-line conditions" *IEEE Transactions on Human Factors in Electronics* 8 (1) 33–48

G Greenberg D P, 1974 "Computer graphics in architecture" *Scientific American* 230 (5) 98–106

Gregory S A, 1964 "The development of an automatic adsorption drier" *The Chemical Engineer* December, 293–302

Gregory S A (Ed.), 1966 *The Design Method* (Butterworth, London)

Habraken N J, 1972 *Supports: An Alternative to Mass Housing* (The Architectural Press, London)

Herskowitz G J, Sankaran M, 1969 "Student experience with interactive computer programs for linear circuit design" *IEEE Transactions on Education* 12 (3) 208–212

Heyerdahl T, 1971 *The Ra Expeditions* (Allen and Unwin, London)

I Hoskins E, 1972 "OXSYS—an integrated computer-aided building system for Oxford method" *Proceedings of the International Conference on Computers in Architecture, York* (British Computer Society, London) pp 275–285

Hoskins E, 1973 "Computer aids for system building" *Industrialization Forum* 4 (5) 27–42

Jones J C, 1963 "A method of sytematic design" in *Conference on Design Methods* Eds J C Jones, D Thornley (Pergamon Press, Oxford) pp 53–73

Jones J C, 1966 "Design methods reviewed" in *The Design Method* Ed. S Gregory (Butterworth, London) pp 295-309

Jones J C, 1967 "Trying to design the future" *Design* number 225, 35-38

Jones J C, 1970 *Design Methods* (John Wiley, Chichester)

Jones J C, Thornley D (Eds), 1963 *Conference on Design Methods* (Pergamon Press, Oxford)

Jungk R, 1976 Interview (by T Durham) in *Radical Technology* Eds G Boyle, P Harper (Wildwood, London)

G Kahn L (Ed.), 1973 *Shelter* (Shelter Publications, Bolinas, Calif.)

I Kamnitzer P, 1969 "Computer aid to design" *Architectural Design* September, 507-508

J Kernohan D, Rankin G, Wallace G, Walters R, 1971 "Relationship models: analytical techniques for design problem solving" Architecture and Building Aids Computer Unit, OP-17, University of Strathclyde, Glasgow, Scotland; *Architectural Design,* 1973, May, 275-278

J Krejcirik M, Sipler V, 1965 "Use of computers for determining the optimum development pattern for a residential area" Building Research Station Library Communication 1235, Building Research Station, Garston, Merseyside, England

Lee K, Stewart C D, 1972 "ARK 2—An implemented computer aided design sytem" *Proceedings of the International Conference on Computers in Architecture, York* (British Computer Society, London) pp 261-266

Levin P H, 1966a "The design process in planning" *Town Planning Review* 37 (1) 5-20

Levin P H, 1966b "Decision-making in urban design" Building Research Station Note 51/66, Building Research Station, Garston, Herts, England

I Lew I P, Brown P H, 1970 "Evaluation and modification of CRAFT for an architectural methodology" in *Emerging Methods in Environmental Design and Planning* Ed. G Moore (MIT Press, Cambridge, Mass.) pp 155-161

Licklider J C R, 1960 "Man-computer symbiosis" *IRE Transactions on Human Factors in Electronics* 1 (1) 4-11

Licklider J C R, 1965 "Man-computer partnership" *International Science and Technology* May, 18-26

Luckman J, 1967 "An approach to the management of design" *Operational Research Quarterly* 18 (4) 345-358

McLuhan M, 1964 *Understanding Media* (Routledge and Kegan Paul, London)

Marcuse H, 1964 *One-dimensional Man* (Routledge and Kegan Paul, London)

Markus T A, 1967 "The role of building performance measurement and appraisal in design method" *The Architects' Journal* 20 December, 1567-1573

Marples D L, 1960 *The Decisions of Engineering Design* (Institute of Engineering Designers, London)

F Maver T W, 1970 "A theory of architectural design in which the role of the computer is identified" *Building Science* 4 199-207

I Maver T W, 1971 "PACE 1: an on-line design facility' *The Architects' Journal* 28 July, 207-214

I Maver T W, 1972 "The space-time interface" *Architectural Design* January, 44-46

Meager M A, 1972 "Computer aids in hospital building" in *Proceedings of the International Conference on Computers in Architecture, York* (British Computer Society, London) pp 181-190

Michie D, Fleming J G, Oldfield J V, 1968 "A comparison of heuristic, interactive, and unaided methods of solving a shortest-route problem" in *Machine Intelligence 3* Ed. D Michie (Edinburgh University Press, Edinburgh) pp 245-255

Miller R B, 1968 "Response time in man-computer conversational transactions" *AFIPS Conference Proceedings* 33 267-277

Miller R B, 1969 "Archetypes in man-computer problem solving" *Ergonomics* **12** (4) 559-581

I Milne M, 1970 "CLUSTER: a structure-finding algorithm" in *Emerging Methods in Environmental Design and Planning* Ed. G Moore (MIT Press, Cambridge, Mass.) pp 126-132

H Mitchell W J, 1972 "Experiments with participation-oriented computer systems" in *Design Participation* Ed. N Cross (Academy Editions, London) pp 73-78

Mitchell W J, 1974 "An approach to automated generation of minimum cost dwelling unit plans" Department of Architecture, University of California, Los Angeles (mimeo)

J Mitchell W J, Steadman P, Liggett R S, 1976 "Synthesis and optimization of small rectangular floor plans" *Environment and Planning B* **3** (1) 37-70

Montagu A, Snyder S, 1972 *Man and the Computer* (Auerbach, Philadelphia)

Moonman E, 1971 "Computer chaos" *New Society* 3 June, 954-955

D Moore G T (Ed.), 1970 *Emerging Methods in Environmental Design and Planning* (MIT Press, Cambridge, Mass.)

J Moseley L, 1963 "A rational design theory for the planning of buildings based on the analysis and solution of circulation problems" *The Architects' Journal* 11 November, 525-537

I Mountford D H, 1974 "BIBRACS—An integrated computer system for architectural use" *CAD 74—Proceedings of the Conference on Computer-Aided Design, London* Eds G W Jones, D R Smith (IPC Science and Technology Press, Guildford)

Mumford E, Banks O, 1967 *The Computer and the Clerk* (Routledge and Kegan Paul, London)

A Negroponte N, 1970 *The Architecture Machine* (MIT Press, Cambridge, Mass.)

G Negroponte N, 1972 "Aspects of living in an architecture machine" in *Design Participation* Ed. N Cross (Academy Editions, London) pp 63-67

B Negroponte N, 1975 *Soft Architecture Machines* (MIT Press, Cambridge, Mass.)

I Negroponte N, Groisser L, 1970 "URBAN 5: a machine that discusses urban design" in *Emerging Methods in Environmental Design and Planning* Ed. G Moore (MIT Press, Cambridge, Mass.) pp 105-114

Newell A, 1965 "Limitations of the current stock of ideas about problem solving" in *Electronic Information Handling* Eds A Kent, O Taulbee (Spartan Books, Washington, DC) pp 195-207

Nickerson R S, 1969 "Man-computer interaction: a challenge for human factors research" *Ergonomics* **12** (4) 501-517

Page J K, 1963 "A review of the papers presented at the conference" in *Conference on Design Methods* Eds J C Jones, D Thornley (Pergamon Press, Oxford) pp 205-215

Papanek V, 1972 *Design for the Real World* (Thames and Hudson, London)

I Paterson J W, 1974 "An integrated CAD system for an architect's department" *Computer Aided Design* **6** (1) 25-31

Peters B, 1972 "Computer applications in the design and build process by West Sussex County Council" *Proceedings of the International Conference on Computers in Architecture, York* (British Computer Society, London) pp 309-316

Porter W, Lloyd K, Fleisher A, 1970 "DISCOURSE: a language and system for computer-assisted city design" in *Emerging Methods in Environmental Design and Planning* Ed. G Moore (MIT Press, Cambridge, Mass.) pp 92-104

Radford R, 1974 "The Harness hospital development programme" *Building International* **7** (1) 43-56

I Ray-Jones A, 1968 "Computer development in West Sussex" *The Architects' Journal* 21 and 28 February, 421-426, 489-493

I Renfrow N, 1976 "ARK 2" *Bulletin of CAAD* number 20, 16-25

RIBA, 1967 *Plan of Work* (Royal Institute of British Architects, London)

[I] Richens P, 1974 "OXSYS—Computer-aided building for oxford method" *CAD 74—Proceedings of the Conference on Computer-Aided Design, London* Eds G W Jones, D R Smith (IPC Science and Technology Press, Guildford)

Roszak T, 1970 *The Making of a Counter-culture* (Faber and Faber, London)

Roszak T, 1972 *Where the Wasteland Ends* (Faber and Faber, London)

Sackman H, 1967 *Computers, System Science and Evolving Society* (John Wiley, New York)

Sackman H, 1970 *Man–Computer Problem-solving* (Auerbach, Philadelphia)

Sass M, Wilkinson W (Eds), 1965 *Computer Augmentation of Human Reasoning* (Spartan Books, Washington, DC)

Schatzoff M, Tsao R, Wiig R, 1967 "An experimental comparison of time-sharing and batch-processing" *Communications, Association for Computing Machinery* 10 (5) 262-265

Scherr A L, 1966 "Time-sharing measurement" *Datamation* 12 (4) 22-26

Schon D A, 1969 "Design in the light of the year 2000" *Student Technologist* (Autumn) 20-24 [Extracts reprinted in Cross N, Elliott D, Roy R (Eds), 1974 *Man-made Futures* (Hutchinson, London) pp 255-263]

Schon D A, 1971 *Beyond the Stable State* (Temple Smith, London)

Shackel B, Shipley P, 1970 *Man–Computer Interaction: A Review of Ergonomics Literature and Related Research* (EMI Electronics Ltd, Feltham, Middx)

Shaffer L H, 1965 "Problem solving on a stochastic process" *Ergonomics* 8 (2) 181-192

Shaw J C, 1964 "JOSS: a designer's view of an experimental on-line computing system" *AFIPS Conference Proceedings* 26 455-463

Shaw J C, 1965 "JOSS: experience with an experimental computing service for use at remote typewriter consoles" P-3149, Rand Corporation, Santa Monica, Calif.

[I] Shirley E, 1974 "Circulation analysis and lift placing in hospitals" *Computer Aided Design* 6 (4) 206-210

Singleton W T, 1966 "Current trends towards systems design" *Ergonomics for Industry* number 12 (HMSO, London)

Singleton W T, 1974 *Man–Machine Systems* (Penguin Books, Harmondsworth)

Smith L B, 1967 "A comparison of batch processing and instant turnaround" *Communications, Association for Computing Machinery* 10 495-500

[B] Souder J J, Clark W E, Elkind J J, Brown M B, 1964 *Planning for Hospitals* (American Hospital Association, Chicago)

Stabler G M, 1967 *Computer-aided Room-Layout Design* unpublished MSc dissertation, University of Manchester Institute of Science and Technology, Manchester, England

[J] Steadman P, 1970 "The automatic generation of minimum-standard house plans" WP-23, Land Use and Built Form Studies, University of Cambridge, Cambridge, England

Stewart C D, Lee K, 1971 "The ARK 2 system" *Progressive Architecture* July, 64-73

[I] Th'ng R, Davies M, 1975 "SPACES" *Computer Aided Design* 7 (2) 112-118

Thompson B, Hughes J, 1974 "An experimental investigation of the performance of a computer-aided building design system" *Proceedings of IFIP Congress 74* (International Federation of Information Processing Societies, Stockholm)

Thring M W, 1973 *Man, Machines and Tomorrow* (Routledge and Kegan Paul, London)

Toffler A, 1970 *Future Shock* (Bodley Head, London)

Vaughan W S, Schumacher-Mavor A, 1972 "Behavioural characteristics of men in the performance of some decision-making task components" *Ergonomics* 15 (3) 267-277

Weeks J, 1965 "Indeterminate architecture" *Transactions of the Bartlett Society* 2 (University College London)

Weinzapfel G, Handel S, 1975 "IMAGE: computer assistant for architectural design" in *Spatial Synthesis in Computer-Aided Building Design* Ed. C M Eastman (Applied Science Publishers, London) pp 61-97

Weinzapfel G, Johnson T, 1972 "The image system and its role in design" *Proceedings of the International Conference on Computers in Architecture, York* (British Computer Society, London) pp 210-217

J Whitehead B, 1970 "The application of analytical techniques to building layout planning" *BUILD International* May, 151-155

I Whitehead B, Eldars M Z, 1964 "An approach to the optimum layout of single storey buildings" *The Architects' Journal* 17 June, 1373-1380

I Whitehead B, Eldars M Z, 1965 "The planning of single-storey layouts" *Building Science* 1 (2) 127-139

Whitfield D, 1967 "Human skill as a determinate of allocation of function" in *The Human Operator in Complex Systems* Eds W T Singleton, R S Easterby, D Whitfield (Taylor and Francis, London) pp 54-60

I Willey D S, 1976 "Approaches to computer-aided architectural sketch design" *Computer Aided Design* 8 (3) 181-186

I Willoughby T, 1970 "Computer aided design of a university campus" *The Architects' Journal* 25 March, 753-758

I Willoughby T, Paterson W, Drummond G, 1970 "Computer-aided architectural planning" *Operational Research Quarterly* 21 (1) 91-98

Woodruff R, 1969 "Industrial application of computer graphics" in *Computer Graphics in Architecture and Design* Ed. M Milne (Yale School of Art and Architecture, New Haven, Conn.) pp 15-22

Yershov A P, 1965 "One view of man-machine interaction" *Journal of the Association for Computing Machinery* 12 15-325

Yntema, D B, Morfield M, Wiesen R, Grossberg M, 1969 "Effect of response delay on on-line problem-solving" *Proceedings of the IEEE/ERS International Symposium on Man-Machine Systems, Cambridge* (Ergonomics Research Society, London)

Yntema D B, Torgerson W S, 1961 "Man-computer cooperation in decisions requiring common sense" *IRE Transactions on Human Factors in Electronics* 2 (1) 20-26

A guide to the literature in computer-aided architectural design. The references marked ● are cited in the text.

A. Books providing a generalized approach to the topic
●Auger B, 1972 *The Architect and the Computer* (Pall Mall Press, London)
●Broadbent G, 1973 *Design in Architecture* (John Wiley, Chichester) chapter 15
●Campion D, 1968 *Computers in Architectural Design* (Elsevier, London)
 Gutteridge B, Wainwright J R, 1973 *Computers in Architectural Practice* (Crosby Lockwood Staples, London)
●Negroponte N, 1970 *The Architecture Machine* (MIT Press, Cambridge, Mass.)

B. Books dealing with more specialized approaches
●Eastman C M (Ed.), 1975 *Spatial Synthesis in Computer-aided Building Design* (Applied Science Publishers, London)
●Negroponte N, 1975 *Soft Architecture Machines* (MIT Press, Cambridge, Mass.)
●Souder J J, Clark W E, Elkind J J, Brown M B, 1964 *Planning for Hospitals* (American Hospital Association, Chicago)

C. Conferences devoted exclusively to computers in architecture. (Individual papers from these conferences are not cited separately in this bibliography.)
 Boston Architectural Center, 1964 *Architecture and the Computer—Proceedings of the First Boston Architectural Center Conference* (Boston Architectural Center, Boston, Mass.)
 British Computer Society, 1972 *International Conference on Computers in Architecture, York* (British Computer Society, London)
 Daru M (Ed.), 1971 *Computer-aided Architectural Design* (Bouwcentrum, Rotterdam)

D. Other major conferences with substantial sections on computer-aided architectural design. (Individual papers from these conferences are cited separately in Sections F-J)
●Cross N (Ed.), 1972 *Design Participation—Proceedings of the Design Research Society Conference, Manchester* (Academy Editions, London)
 Jones G W, Smith D R (Eds), 1974 *CAD 74—Proceedings of the Conference on Computer Aided Design, London* (IPC Science and Technology Press, Guildford)
 Milne M (Ed.), 1969 *Computer Graphics in Architecture and Design—Proceedings of the Yale Conference* (Yale University School of Art and Architecture, New Haven, Conn.)
 Mitchell W J (Ed.), 1972 *Environmental Design: Research and Practice— Proceedings of the Environmental Design Research Association Conference, Los Angeles* (University of California, Los Angeles)
●Moore G T (Ed.), 1970 *Emerging Methods in Environmental Design and Planning— Proceedings of the Design Methods Group Conference, Cambridge, Mass.* (MIT Press, Cambridge, Mass.)

E. Other edited collections with a significant proportion of contributions on computer-aided architectural design
 Harper G N (Ed.), 1968 *Computer Applications in Architecture and Engineering* (McGraw-Hill, New York)
 Vlietstra J, Wielinga R F (Eds), 1973 *Computer-Aided Design* (North-Holland, Amsterdam)

F. The computer and its role in the design process
●Alexander C, 1965 "The question of computers in design" *Landscape* **14** (3) 6-8
●Alexander C, 1971 "The state of the art in design methods" *DMG Newsletter* **5** (3) 3-7; *DMG-DRS Journal: Design Research and Methods* **7** (2) 133-135, 1973
 Amkrentz J H, 1976 "Cybernetic model of the design process"*Computer Aided Design* **8** (3) 187-192

Berkeley E P, 1968 "Computers for design and design for the computer" *Architectural Forum* **128** (2) 60–65

Bernholtz A, 1968 "Some thoughts on computer role playing and design" *Ekistics* **26** (157) 522–524

Bernholtz A, 1968 "Systematic design by computer" *Architectural and Engineering News* **10** (3) 42–43

Bernholtz A, Bierstone E, 1966 "Computer-augmented design" *Design Quarterly* December, 41–52

•Cross N, Maver T W, 1973 "Computer aids for design participation" *Architectural Design* May, 274

Jones J C, 1966 "Design methods compared 2: tactics" *Design* number 213, 46–52

Krauss R I, 1972 "Improving design decisions: recommendations for a computer system for use by the British Government" in *Environmental Design* Ed. W J Mitchell (University of California, Los Angeles)

Krauss R I, Myer J R, 1968 "Design: a case history—a designer's specification for a computer system", Center for Building Research, Massachusetts Institute of Technology, Cambridge, Mass.

Mallen G L, 1974 "Modelling the design process" in *CAD 74* Eds G W Jones, D R Smith (IPC Science and Technology Press, Guildford)

Manheim M L, 1966 "Role of the computer in the design process" *Building Research* **3** March–April, 13–17

Manheim M L, 1966 "Problem-solving processes in planning and design" *Design Quarterly* December, 31–40

•Maver T W, 1970 "A theory of architectural design in which the role of the computer is identified" *Building Science* **4** 199–207

Negroponte N, 1969 "Towards a humanism through machines" *Architectural Design* September, 511–512

Negroponte N, Groisser L B, 1970 "The semantics of architecture machines" *Architectural Design* September, 466–469

Weinzapfel G, 1973 "It might work, but will it help?" *DMG-DRS Journal: Design Research and Methods* **7** (4) 332–335

G. Computer applications in architectural design: introductions, examples, speculations, and comments

Barrett J, 1965 "Will the computer change the practice of architecture?" *Ekistics* **19** (113) 247–249

Barrett J, 1967 "Computer aided building design: where do we go from here?" *Architectural Record* **141** (4) 219–220

Barrett J, 1968 "Glass box and black box: or can artificial intelligence help solve design problems?" *Architectural Record* **144** (7) 137–138

Bijl A, Renshaw A, 1968 *Application of Computer Graphics to Architectural practice* (Architecture Research Unit, University of Edinburgh, Edinburgh, Scotland)

Campion D, Robey K G, 1965 "Perspective drawing by computer" *Architectural Review* November, 380–386

Carter J, 1973 "Computers and the architect, parts 1–4" *The Architects' Journal* 3 October, 815–819; 10 October, 865–870; 24 October, 1003–1011; 31 October, 1053–1060

Chalmers J, 1975 "Computers and Designers" *Construction* **14** 30–33

•Cross N, 1972 "Impact of computers on the architectural design process" *The Architects' Journal* 22 March, 623–628

Davison J A, 1974 "Towards computer aided design in a private architectural practice" in *CAD 74* Eds. G W Jones, D R Smith (IPC Science and Technology Press, Guildford)

•Department of the Environment, 1969 *Computer-aided Architectural Design* (2 volumes) (Department of the Environment, London)

Eastman C M, 1975 "The use of computers instead of drawings in building design" *American Institute of Architects' Journal* March, 46-50

Fairweather L, 1972 "Computers: where now?" *Architects' Journal* December, 1319-1324

Fenves S J, 1966 "Computer use in building design" *Building Research* 3 March - April, 10-12

•Graham B, 1969 "Computer graphics in architectural practice" in *Computer Graphics in Architecture and Design* Ed. M Milne (Yale University School of Art and Architecture, New Haven, Conn.) pp 23-30

•Greenberg D P, 1974 "Computer graphics in architecture" *Scientific American* **230** (5) 98-106

Hatton D, 1968 "Architectural design by computer" *Systems Building and Design* July, 47-51

Hendren P, 1969 "Simulating architectural forms" in *Computer Graphics in Architecture and Design* Ed. M Milne (Yale University School of Art and Architecture, New Haven, Conn.) pp 37-44

Johnston A S T, 1967 "Computers: the implications for architects" *RIBA Journal* February, 53-54

•Kahn L, 1973 "Smart but not wise" in *Shelter* Ed. L Kahn (Shelter Publications, Bolinas, Calif.) pp 112-114

Kliment S A, 1968 "The computer: what next?" *Architectural and Engineering News* **10** (3) 21

Lansdown J, van Tilborg F, 1974 "An experiment in computer-aided architectural design" in *CAD 74* Eds G W Jones, D R Smith (IPC Science and Technology Press, Guildford)

Laxon W R, Lefevre J J, 1974 "An historical cost benefit analysis of a computer system for architectural design" in *CAD 74* Eds G W Jones, D R Smith (IPC Science and Technology Press, Guildford)

Lindheim R, 1965 "Computers and architecture" *Landscape* **14** (3) 8-11

Maver T W, 1972 "Simulation and solution teams in architectural design" in *Design Participation* Ed. N Cross (Academy Editions, London) pp 79-83

Myer T H, Krauss R I, 1967 "Architectural practice and the computer revolution" *Architectural Design* April, 193-195

•Negroponte N, 1972 "Aspects of living in an architecture machine" in *Design Participation* Ed. N Cross (Academy Editions, London) pp 63-67

Negroponte N, 1974 "Concerning responsive architecture" in *The Responsive House* Ed. E Allen (MIT Press, Cambridge, Mass.) pp 302-305

Paterson J W, 1968 "Using the computer for design" *RIBA Journal* December, 564-565

Purcell P, 1970 "Computer graphics in system building" *Industrialized Building* March, 51-52

Souder J J, Clark W E, 1963 "Computer technology: new tool for planning" *American Institute of Architects' Journal* **40** (4) 97-106

Taylor M, 1968 "Towards computer-aided building design" *RIBA Journal* April, 151-152

Teicholz E D, 1968 "Architecture and the computer" *Architectural Forum* **129** (2) 58-61

H. Reviews and progress reports

Applied Research of Cambridge, 1973 *Computer Aided Building: A Study of Current Trends* (Applied Research of Cambridge, Cambridge, England)

•Bijl A, 1974 "Research in progress: Edinburgh CAAD studies" *Computer Aided Design* **6** (3) 183-186

Campion D, Reynolds T, 1974 "Computers in architecture in the UK" *DMG-DRS Journal: Design Research and Methods* **8** (4) 182-199

Eastman C M, 1975 "Computer applications to architecture in the USA" *Computer Aided Design* **6** (3) 119-124

Maver T W, 1975 "Computers in design: the work of ABACUS" *Architectural Design* February, 118-122

•Mitchell W J, 1972 "Experiments with participation-oriented computer systems" in *Design Participation* Ed. N Cross (Academy Editions, London) pp 73-78

Mitchell W J, 1974 "Computer-aided design and the architecture student in the United States" *DMG-DRS Journal: Design Research and Methods* **8** (4) 210-217

Mitchell W J, 1975 "Techniques of automated design in architecture: a survey and evaluation" *Computing and Urban Society* **1** (1) 49-76

Negroponte N, 1975 "Research in progress: the architecture machine" *Computer Aided Design* **7** (3) 190-195

Negroponte N and others, 1969 "Architecture machine" *Architectural Design* September, 510-513

Pavageau F, 1974 "Current computer applications in the architectural field in France" *DMG-DRS Journal: Design Research and Methods* **8** (4) 207-209

Tohmatsu N, 1974 "Computer applications in architecture—review of Japan" *DMG-DRS Journal: Design Research and Methods* **8** (4) 200-205

I. Generalized description of CAAD programs, systems, and approaches

•Alexander C, 1963 "The determination of components for an Indian village" in *Conference on Design Methods* Eds J C Jones, D Thornley (Pergamon Press, Oxford) 83-114

Bax M F T, Kressner L, Habraken N J, 1973 "Computer aided evaluation of a structure for housing: SAR 70" *Bulletin of CAAD* number 13, 36-41

Bijl A, 1971 "A computer program for designing houses" *Bulletin of CAAD* number 6, 15-23

•Bijl A, Shawcross G, 1975 "Housing site layout system" *Computer Aided Design* **7** (1) 2-10

•Buffa E S, Armour G C, Vollman T E, 1964 "Allocating facilities with CRAFT" *Harvard Business Review* **42** (2) 136-158

Campion D, 1966 "Design simulation by computer" *Architectural Review* **140** (838) 460-464

Chalmers J R, Johnson C W, Thompson B, Webster, G J, 1974 "A computer-aided building design system" in *CAD 74* Eds G W Jones, D R Smith (IPC Science and Technology Press, Guildford)

Charalambides S, Lafue G, 1974 "PAVLOV: a program based on a learning method as an aid to architectural design" *Bulletin of CAAD* number 14, 26-31

Clark W E, Souder J J, 1965 "Planning building by computer" *Architectural and Engineering News* **7** (3) 25-33

•Coleman J R, 1973 "Computer aids for participation in housing design" *Computer Aided Design* **5** (3) 166-170

David B, Rivero V, 1974 "An approach to computer-aided architectural design" in *CAD 74* Eds G W Jones, D R Smith (IPC Science and Technology Press, Guildford)

Davis C F, Kennedy M D, 1970 "EPS: a computer program for the evaluation of problem structure" in *Emerging Methods in Environmental Design and Planning* Ed. G T Moore (MIT Press, Cambridge, Mass.) pp 121-125

Eastman C M, 1972 "General space planner: a system of computer-aided architectural design" in *Environmental Design: Research and Practice* Ed. W J Mitchell (University of California, Los Angeles)

Finrow J, 1974 "User-centered computer design systems: The evolutionary designer" in *The Responsive House* Ed. E Allen (MIT Press, Cambridge, Mass.)pp 163-181

Friedman Y, 1971 "The flatwriter: design by computer" *Progressive Architecture* March, 98-101

Fullenwider D R, 1972 "SP-1: a computerized model for store planning" in *Environmental Design: Research and Practice* Ed. W J Mitchell (University of California, Los Angeles)

Gero J S, James I, 1972 "An experiment in a computer-aided constraint-oriented approach to the design of home units" in *Environmental Design: Research and Practice* Ed. W J Mitchell (University of California, Los Angeles) pp

Hamlyn A D, Besant C B, Jeff A, Grant R M, 1974 "An integrated architectural CAD system" in *CAD 74* Eds G W Jones, D R Smith (IPC Science and Technology Press, Guildford)

•Hoskins E, 1973 "Computer aids for system building" *Industrialization Forum* 4 (5) 27-42

Johnson T and others, 1969 "Space arrangement" *Architectural Design* September, 509

•Kamnitzer P, 1969 "Computer aid to design" *Architectural Design* September, 507-508

Kernohan D, Rankin G, Wallace G, Walters R, 1974 "PHASE: an interactive appraisal package for whole hospital design" in *CAD 74* Eds G W Jones, D R Smith (IPC Science and Technology Press, Guildford)

Laing L, 1975 "A computer simulation model for the design of airport terminal buildings" *Computer Aided Design* 7 (1) 37-42

Laing L, Gentles J C, 1975 "A flexible computer simulation model of airport terminal buildings as an aid during the whole design process" *DMG-DRS Journal: Design Research and Methods* 9 (3) 288-293

Lee R C, Moore J M, 1967 "CORELAP: computerized relationship layout planning" *Journal of Industrial Engineering* 18 (3) 195-200

Lesniak Z K, Grodzki Z, Winiarski M S, 1975 "Optimisation of industrialised building systems" *Building Science* 10 (3) 169-175

•Lew I P, Brown P H, 1970 "Evaluation and modification of CRAFT for an architectural methodology" in *Emerging Methods in Environmental Design and Planning* Ed. G T Moore (MIT Press, Cambridge, Mass.) pp 155-161

Main A, 1974 "Interactive building design" in *CAD 74* Eds G W Jones, D R Smith (IPC Science and Technology Press, Guildford)

Mathur K S, 1974 "CASH: A computer aided design tool for housing" in *CAD 74* Eds G W Jones, D R Smith (IPC Science and Technology Press, Guildford)

Mathur K S, 1975 "CUPID: a computer game" *Architectural Design* September, 595-598

•Maver T W, 1971 "PACE 1: an on-line design facility" *Architects' Journal* 28 July, 207-214

Maver T W, 1972 "PACE 1: an on-line design facility" in *Environmental Design: Research and Practice* Ed. W J Mitchell (University of California, Los Angeles)

•Maver T W, 1972 "The space-time interface" *Architectural Design* January, 44-46

•Milne M, 1970 "CLUSTER: a structure-finding algorithm" in *Emerging Methods in Environmental Design and Planning* Ed. G Moore (MIT Press, Cambridge, Mass.) pp 126-132

•Mountford D H, 1974 "BIBRACS: an integrated computer system for architectural use" in *CAD 74* Eds G W Jones, D R Smith (IPC Science and Technology Press, Guildford)

Negroponte N, 1967 "URBAN5: an on-line design partner" *Ekistics* 24 (142) 289–291

Negroponte N, 1969 "URBAN5: an experimental urban design partner" in *Computer Graphics in Architecture and Design* Ed. M Milne (Yale University School of Art and Architecture, New Haven, Conn.) pp 77–88

•Negroponte N, Groisser L B, 1970 "URBAN5: a machine that discusses urban design" in *Emerging Methods in Environmental Design and Planning* Ed. G T Moore (MIT Press, Cambridge, Mass.) pp 105–114

Negroponte N, Groisser L B, Taggart J, 1972 "HUNCH: an experiment in sketch recognition" in *Environmental Design: Research and Practice* Ed. W J Mitchell (University of California, Los Angeles)

Newman W M, 1972 "Graphics system for computer-aided design" in *Environmental Design: Research and Practice* Ed. W J Mitchell (University of California, Los Angeles)

Newman W M, 1966 "An experimental program for architectural design" *Computer Journal* 9 (1) 21–26

Noble J, Turner J, 1971 "Evaluating housing layouts by computer" *The Architects' Journal* 10 February, 315–318

Parsons J W, Chalmers J R, 1970 "The development of a computer aided design system for a large scale user" *Proceedings of the IEE Conference on Man–Computer Interaction, Teddington* pp 160–165

•Paterson J W, 1974 "An integrated CAD system for an architect's department" *Computer Aided Design* 6 (1) 25–31

Porter W, et al, 1969 "Discourse and choice" *Architectural Design* September, 510

Portlock P C, Whitehead B, 1971 "A program for practical layout planning" *Building Science* 6 (3) 214

Purcell P, Chalmers J, 1972 "The CEDAR system" in *Environmental Design: Research and Practice* Ed. W J Mitchell (University of California, Los Angeles)

•Ray-Jones A, 1968 "Computer development in West Sussex" *The Architects' Journal* 21 February, 421–426; 28 February, 489–493

•Renfrow N, 1976 "ARK 2" *Bulletin of CAAD* number 20, 16–25

•Richens P, 1974 "OXSYS: computer-aided building for Oxford method" in *CAD 74* Eds G W Jones, D R Smith (IPC Science and Technology Press, Guildford)

Seehof J M, Evans W D, 1967 "Automated layout design program" *Journal of Industrial Engineering* 18 (12) 690–695

•Shirley E, 1974 "Circulation analysis and lift placing in hospitals" *Computer Aided Design* 6 (4) 206–210

Stewart C D, Lee K, 1971 "The ARK 2 system" *Progressive Architecture* July, 64–73

Stewart C D, Lee K, 1972 "Comprospace: interactive computer graphics in the real world" in *Environmental Design: Research and Practice* Ed. W J Mitchell (University of California, Los Angeles)

Th'ng R, 1974 "A rationalized approach towards architectural design" in *CAD 74* Eds G W Jones, D R Smith (IPC Science and Technology Press, Guildford)

Th'ng R, 1975 "Can computer aids assist towards contributing a systematic approach for architectural designers in practice? Yes" *DMG-DRS Journal: Design Research and Methods* 9 (3) 200–205

•Th'ng R, Davies M, 1975 "SPACES: an integrated suite of computer programs for accommodation scheduling, layout generation and appraisal of schools" *Computer Aided Design* 7 (2) 112–118

Vollman T E, Nugent C E, Zantier R L, 1968 "Computerized model for office layout" *Journal of Industrial Engineering* **19** (7) 321-327

●Whitehead B, Eldars M Z, 1964 "An approach to the optimum layout of single storey buildings" *The Architects' Journal* 17 June, 1373-1380

●Whitehead B, Eldars M Z, 1965 "The planning of single-storey layouts" *Building Science* **1** (2) 127-139

●Willey D S, 1976 "Approaches to computer-aided architectural sketch design" *Computer Aided Design* **8** (3) 181-186

●Willoughby T, 1970 "Computer-aided design of a university campus" *The Architects' Journal* 25 March, 753-758

●Willoughby T, Paterson W, Drummond G, 1970 "Computer-aided architectural planning" *Operational Research Quarterly* **21** (1) 91-98

Windheim L S, Negroponte N, Flanders S, 1972 "Computer-aided hospital design" in *Environmental Design: Research and Practice* Ed. W J Mitchell (University of California, Los Angeles)

J. Specialist descriptions, research reports, and theoretical foundations

Agraa O M, Whitehead B, 1968 "A study of movement in a school building" *Building Science* **2** 279-289

Aguilar R J, Hand J E, 1968 "A generalized linear model for optimization of architectural planning" *American Federation of Information Processing Societies, Spring Joint Computer Conference* **32** 81-88

Alexander C, 1963 "HIDECS 3: four computer programs for the hierarchical decomposition of systems which have an associated graph" Research Report R63-27 Civil Engineering Systems Laboratory, Massachusetts Institute of Technology, Cambridge, Mass.

●Alexander C, Manheim M, 1962 "HIDECS 2: a computer program for the hierarchical decomposition of a set with an associated graph" publication 160 Civil Enginerring Systems Laboratory, Massachusetts Institute of Technology, Cambridge, Mass

Archer L B, 1963 "Planning accommodation for hospitals and the transportation problem technique" *The Architects' Journal* 17 July, 139-142

●Berger S R, Briggs M P, Gill R, Markovits N, 1974 "The construction and extension of a general decision model and its application to space-planning problems" internal paper, Department of Architecture, University of Bristol, Bristol, England

Bierstone E, Bernholtz A, 1967 "HIDECS-RECOMP procedure" Department of Civil Engineering, Massachusetts Institute of Technology, Cambridge, Mass.

Brotchie J F M, Linzey P T, 1971 "A model for integrated building design" *Building Science* **6** 89-96

Carter D J, Whitehead B, 1975 "Data for generative layout programs" *Building Science* **10** 95-102

Carter D J, Whitehead B, 1975 "The use of cluster analysis in multi-storey layout planning" *Building Science* **10** 287-296

●Cross N, Eastham L, Morton M, 1970 "Computer-aided information retrieval: a pilot study of some possibilities" *Building* 11 September, 127-131

Curtis D, 1974 "Interactive graphics as an aid to building design" in *CAD 74* Eds G W Jones, D R Smith (IPC Science and Technology Press, Guildford)

David A, Noviant P, Roucairol C, 1973 "A global spatial localization of activities method" *Bulletin of CAAD* number 13, 7-13

Eastman C M, 1973 "Automated space planning" *Artificial Intelligence* **4** (7) 41-64

Eastman C M, 1976 "General purpose building description systems" *Computer Aided Design* **8** (1) 17-26

Eastman C M, Schwartz M, 1973 "Methods for treating variable shaped objects in computer aided design" *Bulletin of CAAD* number 13, 19-28

England R, 1972 "Planning complex building systems" *Architectural Research and Teaching* **2** (1) 34-39

Fair G R, Flowerdew A, Munro W, Rowley D, 1966 "Note on the computer as an aid to the architect" *Computer Journal* **9** (1) 16-20

Filmer R M, 1974 "Optimization as a design tool" in *CAD 74* Eds G W Jones, D R Smith (IPC Science and Technology Press, Guildford)

Frew R S, Ragade R K, Roe P H, 1972 "The animals of architecture" in *Environmental Design: Research and Practice* Ed. W J Mitchell (University of California, Los Angeles)

Grason J, 1970 "A dual linear graph representation for space-filling location problems of the floor plan type" in *Emerging Methods in Environmental Design and Planning* Ed. G T Moore (MIT Press, Cambridge, Mass.) pp 170-178

Gray J C, 1974 "Software structures for computer-aided building" in *CAD 74* Eds G W Jones, D R Smith (IPC Science and Technology Press, Guildford)

Hafez E, Agraa O M, Whitehead B, 1967 "Automation of data preparation in computer programs for the planning of single storey layouts" *Building Science* **2** 83-88

Hormann A M, 1972 "Machine-aided evaluation of alternative designs" in *Environmental Design: Research and Practice* Ed. W J Mitchell (University of California, Los Angeles)

•Kernohan D, Rankin G, Wallace G, Walters R, 1973 "Relationship models: analytical techniques for design problem solving" *Architectural Design* May, 275-278

Krejcirik M, 1969 "Computer-aided plant layout" *Computer Aided Design* **2** (1) 7-19

•Krejcirik M, Sipler V, 1965 "Use of computers for determining the optimum development pattern for a residential area" Building Research Station Library Communication number 1235, Building Research Station, Garston, Merseyside, England

Laxon W R, 1974 "Grafting interactive graphics onto an existing batch system for architectural design" in *CAD 74* Eds G W Jones, D R Smith (IPC Science and Technological Press, Guildford)

Liggett R S, 1972 "Floor plan layout by implicit enumeration" in *Environmental Design: Research and Practice* Ed. W J Mitchell (University of California, Los Angeles)

Mitchell W J, 1975 "The theoretical foundation of computer-aided architectural design" *Environment and Planning B* **2** (2) 127-150

Mitchell W J, Dillon R, 1972 "A polyomino assembly procedure for architectural floor planning" in *Environmental Design: Research and Practice* Ed. W J Mitchell (University of California, Los Angeles)

•Mitchell W J, Steadman P, Liggett R S, 1976 "Synthesis and optimization of small rectangular floor plans" *Environment and Planning B* **3** (1) 37-70

Mohr M, 1972 "A computer model of the design process that uses a concept of an apartment floor plan to solve layout problems" in *Environmental Design: Research and Practice* Ed. W J Mitchell (University of California, Los Angeles)

•Moseley L, 1963 "A rational design theory for the planning of buildings based on the analysis and solution of circulation problems" *The Architects' Journal* 11 November, 525-537

Payne I, 1973 "Multidimensional scaling in environmental research" *Architectural Science Review* **16** (3) 155-162

Pereira L M, Portas M, Monteiro L F, Periera F, 1974 "Interactive dimensional layout schemes from adjacency graphs" *Bulletin of CAAD* number 14, 21-25

Philips R J, 1969 "Computerized approaches to circulation" *Building* 18 April, 117-122

Portlock P C, Whitehead B, 1974 "Three dimensional layout planning" *Building Science* **9** (1) 45

•Steadman P, 1970 "The automatic generation of minimum-standard house plans" WP-23, Land Use and Built Form Studies, University of Cambridge, Cambridge, England

Steadman P, 1973 "Graph theoretic representation of architectural arrangement" *Architectural Research and Teaching* **2** (3) 161–172

Tabor O P, 1969 "Traffic in buildings 1: pedestrian circulation" WP-17, Land Use and Built Form Studies, University of Cambridge, Cambridge, England

Tabor O P, 1970 "Traffic in buildings 2: systematic activity-location" WP-18, Land Use and Built Form Studies University of Cambridge, Cambridge, England

Teague L C, 1970 "Network models of configurations of rectangular parallelepipeds" in *Emerging Methods in Environmental Design and Planning* Ed. G T Moore (MIT Press, Cambridge, Mass.) pp 162–169

Teague L C, 1968 "Representation of spatial relationships in a computer system for building design" Research Report number R68-25, Civil Engineering Systems Laboratory, Massachusetts Institute of Technology, Cambridge, Mass.

Teicholz E D, 1974 "Computer aided space planning" Laboratory for Computer Graphics and Spatial Analysis, Harvard University, Cambridge, Mass.

White D S, 1972 "Mathematical evaluation and optimization of the three dimensional hospital layout problem" in *Environmental Design: Research and Practice* Ed. W J Mitchell, University of California, Los Angeles

•Whitehead B, 1970 "The application of analytical techniques to building layout planning" *BUILD International* May, 151–155

Willoughby T M, 1975 "Building forms and circulation patterns" *Environment and Planning B* **2** (1) 59–87

Yessios C I, 1972 "FOSPLAN: a formal space planning language" in *Environmental Design: Research and Practice* Ed. W J Mitchell (University of California, Los Angeles)

Yessios C I, 1974 "Site planning with SIPLAN" *Bulletin of CAAD* number 14, 1–9

K. Program catalogues

Hutton G, Rostron R M, 1974 *Computer Programs for the Building Industry, 1974* (Hutton and Rostron/The Architectural Press/McGraw-Hill, London)

Lee K, 1974 *Computer Programs in Environmental Design* (Environmental Design and Research Center, Boston, Mass.)

Stewart C D, Teicholz E D, Lee K, 1970 *Computer Architecture Programs* (Center for Environmental Research, Boston, Mass)

Author index

Adams J 67
Alexander C 7, 8, 11, 12, 24, 29, 30, 32, 58, 71
Archer L B 12, 21, 22, 59, 140
Asimow M 12, 15, 16, 18, 21, 22
Auger B 4, 39, 40, 114, 119, 120

Babbage C 138
Banks O 112, 120, 121
Bazjanac V 69–71, 95
Beaumont M J 72
Bell D 4
Berger S 132
Boguslaw R 142, 143
Broadbent G 4, 9, 16, 17, 33
Buffa E S 72

Cakin S 41, 123
Campion D 4
Carbonell J R 66
Chalmers J 25, 40, 114
Chermayeff S 30
Cohen L 67
Coleman J R 124
Cooley M 113–115, 119
Le Corbusier 3
Cross N 4, 107–109, 111–113, 119, 122

Davies M 56, 118
Davis R M 64
Derbyshire M E 118

Eastman C M 33, 59
Eberhard J P 58
Eldars M Z 33, 35–38, 71, 72, 86, 89
Ellul J 4
Erikson W J 67
Esher, Lord 116
Esherick J 143, 144
Evans B 107, 110, 124, 125

Fano R M 64
Fitts P 134

Galbraith J K 4
Gero J S 137
Gibbon M 106
Gold M 68
Goodman R 4
Grant E E 66
Greenberg D P 45, 46
Gregory S A 16, 20, 21
Groisser L 43, 56, 71

Habraken N J 4
Handel S 131
Herskowitz G J 67
Heyerdahl T 6, 7
Hughes J 119, 130

Jones J C 4–6, 12–14, 17, 18, 106, 107, 140
Julian W G 137
Jungk R 138

Kahn L 59
Kamnitzer P 41, 45
Kernohan D 32
Krejcirik M 71

Levin P H 17–19, 139
Licklider J C R 63–65
Llewellyn-Davies, Lord 116
Lovelace, Lady 138
Luckman J 14, 18, 19, 32, 37, 133

McLuhan M 4
Manheim M 30
Marcuse H 4
Markus T A 14, 21
Marples D L 19, 20
Maver T W 41, 42, 71, 117, 119, 122, 123
Meager M A 26
Michie D 70, 71, 95, 138
Miller R B 66, 142
Milne M 30–32, 71
Mitchell W J 37, 123
Montagu A 105
Moonman E 58
Moore G T 17, 24
Moseley L 33, 71
Mumford E 112, 120, 121

Negroponte N 3, 4, 43, 56–58, 63, 64, 71, 125, 138
Newell A 64, 138
Nickerson R S 65, 66

Page J K 12, 14
Papanek V 140
Paterson J W 27, 28

Radford R 26
Ramo S 143
Ray-Jones A 27
Roszak T 4, 143

Sackman H 65, 66, 115
Sankaran M 67
Sass M 64
Schatzoff M 67
Scherr A L 65
Schon D A 4, 5
Schumacher-Mavor A 65, 138, 139
Shackel B 65
Shaffer L H 69-71
Shaw J C 64, 65
Shipley P 65
Shirley E 132
Singleton W T 133, 135, 136, 140
Sipler V 71
Skidmore, Owings and Merrill 69
Smith L B 67
Snyder S 105
Souder J J 44, 71
Stabler G M 72, 75, 76
Steadman P 37

Talbot R J 77
Th'ng R 56

Thompson B 119, 130
Thornley D 4, 12
Thring M W 119
Toffler A 4
Torgerson W S 65

Vaughan W S 65, 138, 139
Voyer R 106

Ward A 4, 16
Weeks J 4
Weinzapfel G 131
Whitehead B 33-38, 71-73, 86, 89
Whitfield D 137
Wilkinson W 64
Willey D S 130
Willoughby T 38, 71, 89
Woodruff R 123

Yershov A P 64
Yntema D B 65, 66

Subject index

ABACUS (Architecture and Building Aids Computer Unit, Strathclyde) 46, 56, 87
Abilities of humans and/or machines (see attributes and performance, comparison of human and machine)
Accommodation scheduling 47, 48, 117, 118
Adaptability of buildings 116, 117, 119 125
AIDA 18, 19, 32, 33, 37, 133
Algorithmic approaches 37, 63, 64
Analysis
  by computer 29-33
  in systematic design 12-14, 21
Anxiety from working with computers (see also stress) 113
Applied Research of Cambridge 34
Appraisal (see evaluation)
Architect (see designer)
Architectural education
  and computer-aided design 125
  and systematic design 16
Architecture Machine 3, 56, 57, 59, 138
Architecture Machine Group 57, 124
ARK 2 148
Artificial intelligence 56, 57, 110, 124, 125
Attributes of humans and/or machines 69, 71, 107, 134-136, 139 (see also performance, comparison of human and machine)
Automation 115, 119

BAID 39, 40, 148
Batch processing 66-68
BIBRACS 148
BOP 69, 148
Briefing 117-119
Building Economics Research Unit 117
Building industry
  changes in 116
  computer system for 121, 122
Building Research Station 121
Building team 121-123, 129

CARD 75-78
CEDAR 25, 29, 40, 114, 119, 130, 131, 149
Change agents 121, 131
Checklist for CAAD systems 144-147
Circulation
  as basis for design 33, 73
  in room-layout problem 72, 73
  simulation of 43, 44

City-Scape 44-46, 123, 149
Client
  implications of CAD for 3, 118
  relationship with architect 118
  role in design process 9, 123, 124
CLUSTER 30-32, 149
Computer
  access to 24, 64
  applications of 34, 35, 63, 105, 106, 112, 113
  attitudes towards 24, 58
  criticisms of role in design 57-59
  as design aid 3, 4, 17, 24-18, 29-59, 69, 70, 95, 105, 106, 112-125, 130-133, 142, 144
  as problem-solving aid 66-71, 130
Computer graphics 28, 44-46, 58, 113, 138
Computer languages 63, 64
Computer systems (see also systems design)
  in the building industry 109, 121-123
  designers of 66, 131-143 passim
  evaluation of 65-68
  failures of 58
  interactive 64, 65, 130, 137-139
  on-line vs off-line 66-68
  response time in 65, 66
  users of 65, 66, 143, 144
Conferences on design methods 12, 16, 17
COPLANNER 43, 44, 149
CRAFT 150
Creativity 141
Cyclical structure
  of the design process 18, 19

Decisionmaking
  in design 18-21, 139
  by designer 113, 129
  in queuing problem 69
Department of Health and Social Security 26
Department of the Environment 25, 106, 114, 116
Design
  computer-aided 17, 24-28, 29-59, 69-73, 95, 108-125, 129-131, 137, 142, 144
  craft 6-8, 10
  difficulty of 132, 133
  evolutionary 7, 8
  nature of 140-142
  postindustrial 3-6, 10
  professional 8-11
  self-conscious 11
  systematic 12-16, 21, 24

Designer
  and the computer 17, 41, 58,
    108-129 *passim*, 144
  generalist 110, 111, 125
  naive 109-111, 125
  professional 4-8, 123
Design failures 5, 11
Design methods 4, 5, 12-17, 24
Design office 6-8, 115, 119-121
Design problems 140, 141
Design process
  comparisons of in different professions
    21-23
  effects of computers on 116-125, 129,
    130, 143-144
  and industrialization 8-11
  model of 21
  nature of 17-21, 139
  participation in 4, 123-125, 137
  pressures for change in 5, 11, 21, 116,
    117, 129
  research on 17-21
  structure of 18-21
Design research 17, 18
Design team (see building team)
DISCOURSE 150
Drawings
  produced by computer 28, 44, 119
  use of in design 5-7, 9, 28, 116

Effectiveness of computer aids 64-95
  passim, 129-131, 133
Effects
  of computer aids 105, 112-125,
    129-131
  of technological change 105, 106
Evaluation
  by computer 40-46, 123, 124
  of computer systems 65-68, 74-95
  lack of 130, 131
  as part of appraisal 42
  in systematic design 12-14, 21, 40, 41
  weakness of 131, 132
Experiments
  lack of evidence from 130-132
  man vs machine 69-71, 74-85
  man vs man-machine vs machine 70,
    71, 85-101, 138
  on-line vs off-line 66-68
  in simulation studies 108-111

Fitts list 134-136, 138
Forecasting
  in technology assessment 106, 107
Form and function in craft design 6, 7

GDM 132, 133, 150
GREET 57
GROPE 57
Guggenheim Museum 142

Harness system 26, 29, 115, 132, 150
Heuristic approaches 63, 64, 70
HIDECS 30, 32, 151
Hierarchical structure
  by Alexander's method 29, 30
  by CLUSTER 30-32
  of the design office 120
  of the design process 19-21
  of systems 140
Hochschule für Gestaltung, Ulm 12, 16
Hospital design
  by COPLANNER 44
  by Harness system 26, 132
  in Whitehead and Eldars example 35

House design
  by AIDA 18, 19, 32, 33, 37
  by BAID 39, 40
  minimum 37
  participation in 124, 137
Human-computer interaction 63-73,
  93-95
Human-machine interface 95, 137, 138
Human-machine systems (see systems
  design)
HUNCH 57

IMAGE 131, 151
Indian village design (Alexander's example)
  12, 24, 29, 30
Industrialization 8, 9
Information retrieval 109, 110, 113
Interaction matrix (see relationship matrix)
INTU-VAL 41, 42

JOSS 64, 65

Kirchoff's laws 37

Lift location in Harness hospital design 132
Look-out institution 106

MAC 64, 65, 68
Machine
    as architect 3, 56-59, 124
    concept of in architectural design
        philosophy 3
Machine intelligence (see artificial
    intelligence)
Management pyramid 119-121
Man-hours, saving of 114
Man-machine (see human-computer and
    human-machine)
Manufacturer 123
Massachusetts Institute of Technology
    (MIT) 17, 24, 56
Method of Systematic Design 12, 13
MDS 32, 49, 151
Minimum house plans 37
Models, in computer-aided architectural
    design 71
Modern Movement (in design) 7
Morphology of design 13-16

Office design, by GDM 132
Office of Technology Assessment 106
Optimum
    difficulty of achieving in design 37
    house plans 37
    identification of optimum option set
        (AIDA) 19
OXSYS 15

PACE 41, 42, 152
Performance
    appraisal of in buildings 42, 44
    comparison of human and machine
        68-72, 80, 85, 91-93, 129,
        132, 134-136
    human 77-92 passim
    human-machine 90, 93-95, 130
    machine 78-80, 91-93, 133
    measures of 77
Postindustrial society 4
Problem finding
    in design 18, 141
Problem solving
    algorithmic and heuristic aspects of
        63-65, 138
    comparison of human and machine
        performances 69-71
    in design 18, 141
    with on-line and off-line computing
        systems 67
Production information 116, 117, 119

Quantity surveyor 122

Ra (papyrus boat) 6, 7
Redundancy (see staff, reduction of)
Relationship matrix (also interaction
    matrix)
    in CLUSTER 30
    in experimental problems 74, 86
    in MDS 32
    in SPACES 48, 49
    in STUNI 38
    in Whitehead and Eldars program 35
RIBA 21, 22
Robot architect (see machine as architect)
Roles
    of humans and machines 133-139
Room layout
    approaches to 72
    by CARD 75, 76
    experimental problems 74, 75, 89, 92
    problem of 33, 72-74, 77, 85
    programs for 33
    by SPACES 48-51
    by STUNI 38, 39
    by Whitehead and Eldars program
        35-37

School design
    CAD experiments with 118, 119
    by SPACES 46-56
SEAC 25, 40
SEE 57
SEEK 57
Semilattice structure
    in CLUSTER 31, 32
Simulation
    of computer-aided design 105-113,
        124, 125
    of construction industry 68
    in evaluation procedures 43-46, 123
Site planning
    by BAID 39, 40
    by STUNI 38, 39
Solution team 123, 124
Space allocation (see room layout)
SPACES 46-56, 118, 152
SSHA 152
Staff
    reduction of 114, 120, 121, 129
    variety of 120, 121
Stress
    in working with computers 108,
        112-115, 129

Structural frame design
  by CEDAR 40, 119, 130, 131
Study carrel design
  in CLUSTER example 30, 31
STUNI 38, 39, 89, 92, 93, 152
Symbiotic partnership 63, 64, 130
Synthesis
  by computer 33-40
  problems for heuristic modelling 71, 72
  in systematic design 12-14, 21
System building 25, 26, 116, 117
System Development Corporation 66
Systematic Method for Designers 13
Systemic testing 106, 107
Systems design 4, 5
  of design 140-144
  human-machine 133-140
  power of 142, 143
Systems design team 143

Tasks associated with computer-aided
  design 114, 115
Technological change 4, 5, 8, 11, 105, 106
Technology assessment 105-107
TELCOMP 64
Threats and promises of computer-aided
  design 115, 125, 126, 144
Time sharing 64-66, 68, 122
Time-Sharing Ltd 64
Tradition
  in craft design 8

Transportation planning
  by INTUVAL 41
Travelling salesman problem 70, 71, 138
Tree structure
  by Alexander's method 29, 30
  of the design process 18, 19, 32
TSS 66, 67
Two-dimensional structure
  of the design process 21

University design
  in STUNI example 38, 39
University of Manchester Institute of
  Science and Technology 75
University of Strathclyde 86
University of Sydney 137
Urban design
  by City-Scape 44, 45
  by URBAN5 43
URBAN5 42, 43, 56, 57, 153
Users
  of buildings 3, 118, 119, 123
  of computer systems 65, 66, 143, 144
  participation by in design 119, 123,
    124, 129

West Sussex system 27, 29, 153
Whitehead and Eldars program 35-37, 39,
  87, 89, 92, 93, 153
Work rate 113, 129